WITH THE DRAGON'S CHILDREN

David J. Garms

Suite 300 - 990 Fort St
Victoria, BC, Canada, V8V 3K2
www.friesenpress.com

Copyright © 2015 by David J. Garms
Second Edition — 2015
First Edition Published in 1973 by Exposition Press, Jericho, New York, USA

Book to be copyright protected with U.S. Library of Congress and in accordance with Canadian copyright laws.

No part of this publication may be reproduced in any form, or by any means, electronic or mechanical, including photocopying, recording, or any information browsing, storage, or retrieval system, without permission in writing from the publisher or author. Short quotations in critical essays and reviews are allowed.

ISBN
978-1-4602-0927-1 (Hardcover)
978-1-4602-0925-7 (Paperback)
978-1-4602-0926-4 (eBook)

1. History, Military, Vietnam War

Distributed to the trade by The Ingram Book Company

[Second Edition]

Table of Contents

With The Dragon's Children	viii
Preface	ix
Introduction	xii
Acknowledgements	xiv
Chapter I The Way to Dragon Land	1
Chapter II A Town in the Delta	18
Chapter III The Men Who Changed Sides	38
Chapter IV Of Hearts and Minds	58
Chapter V "Will You Eat Dog Meat?"	72

With the Dragon's Children

Chapter VI
A Few More Names   82

Chapter VII
Presenting Mr. Cat   110

Chapter VIII
Happy New Year   132

Chapter IX
The Professor Who Went to War   144

Chapter X
Aftermath   158

Appendix I
Chieu Hoi Education Guidelines   160

Appendix II
Endnotes   173

Appendix III
Selected Bibliography   183

About The Author   187

This book is dedicated to my wonderful brother and friend, Dan. We miss you.

With The Dragon's Children

With the Dragon's Children is the first-hand account of interactions with Vietcong who responded to the South Vietnamese government's amnesty program. The narrative, packed with information about Vietnamese attitudes, aspirations, and reactions to the war, explores their rich history and culture, and discusses the operation of the amnesty program.

After valuable experience with the Peace Corps in India and on assignment with AID (U.S. Agency for International Development), the author received intensive instruction in the Vietnamese language and culture.

Assigned to a small province (Go Cong) in the Delta as the civilian U.S. advisor to the amnesty program for the Vietcong, he worked with—and befriended—about one thousand former Vietcong. A fascinating picture of farmers, bureaucrats, soldiers and merchants emerged out of this experience. He also gained insight on gender issues and how the war impacted on women.

Based on extensive notes, unclassified government documents, books, and interviews carried out over a three-year period in Vietnam, *With the Dragon's Children* is the only book written about the U.S. supported amnesty (Chieu Hoi) program for the Vietcong.

Preface

The Vietnamese sometimes call themselves "Children of the Dragon." Many of their legends attribute the beginning of their nation to the mating of a dragon and a fairy in the misty, prehistoric past. The following is a retelling of one such legend:

Many, many years ago, a dragon named Lac Long rose up from his home in the deep sea and walked on land. The land was exquisite, and the animals and plants were varied and abundant.

At the same time, a fairy, who was called Au Co, came down from the misty mountains where she dwelled. She too explored the valleys, the plains, and the forests; their richness evoked a sense of awe within her.

And so the dragon and the fairy chanced to meet, and came together as one. From this union, Au Co gave birth to one hundred children.

However, Lac Long and Au Co could not remain together forever; the dragon had to return to his sea, and the fairy to her mountains. At their parting, Lac Long took fifty of the children to dwell with him, and Au Co took fifty to live with her.

Thus two types of people came to inhabit the land; some dwelt in the mountains, and some lived near the sea. Their ways were disparate, and though conflicts flared up between them, they never forgot their common ancestry.

The descendants of the first one hundred ancestors established the first great kingdom of the land. In memory of their heritage, they called the kingdom Au Lac. The kingdom was eventually destroyed by invaders from the north, but the descendants of Au Lac persevered and established a second kingdom.

The kingdoms of this land were repeatedly invaded and destroyed, but each time the people recovered and rebuilt. Great conflicts raged among the people, but in the end, they reunited and lived together once more in peace. The land had many different names—Au Lac, Van Xuan, Dai Viet, Vietnam—but always the people called themselves "Children of the Dragon."

More than two thousand years ago, the people of the land now called Vietnam said:

> *Mountain and river divide land from land,*
> *But the sun and stars are in the same sky.*
> *And Lac Long and Au Co are not forgotten.*

History cannot support the facts of the legend, but it can support its spirit. The history of Vietnam is the story of a land repeatedly shattered by wars with its neighbors and by wars with itself. To the Vietnamese the destruction, poverty, and oppression caused by war is an ancient story. Despite two thousand years of almost continual conflict, the people have never lost their belief in a common heritage, nor their expectation of a destiny which, in the end, must also be common. In recent history, this shared destiny was realized in 1975 when Vietnam became one nation again.

Little did I realize that the North would take over the South only four years after my departure from Vietnam in

With the Dragon's Children

1971; streets would be named after Ho Chi Minh, and the former capital of South Vietnam (Saigon) would also bear his name.

The full impact of a history of wars with periods of reunification and/or independence influenced the forces that brought about the country becoming one in 1975. Although the country's destiny remains the same, its preservation tools are understandably different today. During the U.S. involvement in the Vietnam War, the Chinese provided munitions and technical and financial support to North Vietnam. Today the roles are reversed. A unified Vietnam is aligning itself with the U.S. as a deterrent against China. The U.S. is expected to provide technical assistance and training to Vietnam while Vietnam may provide U.S. Naval access to the port at Cam Ranh Bay.

Although much has changed in Vietnam since the end of the war, much has remained the same. Therefore, this second edition of *With the Dragon's Children* still has relevance, not only for a retrospective look at the Vietnam War, but also in understanding Vietnam's current economic and foreign policies and appreciating its rich culture, traditions and history.

Introduction

With the Dragon's Children is a personal account of the thirteen months I spent in a Delta town in South Vietnam working with the amnesty program for Vietcong. I was a civilian employed by AID and had been assigned to the U.S. Advisory Team in the province of Go Cong (now called Tien Giang province; the capital of the province is still Go Cong).

From July 1967 to August 1968, I had the opportunity to meet and know and, in some instances, form close friendships with about one thousand former Vietcong. I worked with a number of other individuals assigned directly or indirectly to this particular program, most of whom were Vietnamese, and some of whom had once served in the ranks of the Vietcong. Thus, I was able to develop something of an understanding as to why a rather large number of individuals became part of the Vietcong movement and, conversely, why these same individuals had chosen to abandon it.

When I first arrived in Vietnam, writing a book was the farthest thing from my mind. I began to keep fairly extensive notes—which later became the basis for the book—but at the time I did so entirely for my own interest. I didn't decide to write a book until after I had returned to the United States in 1971.

With the Dragon's Children

The scope of this book is limited in both time and place; between 1967 and 1971 I spent a total of thirty-seven months in South Vietnam, but I have limited the time to one year and limited the place, for the most part, to a single province.

As far as I found it possible to do so, I have restricted the expression of my opinions and values in this book. It is not really *my* story—it is the story of a number of ordinary Vietnamese who happened to be caught up in a war.

Many who served in Vietnam—willingly or not—have feelings toward the people of that country which may differ from my own. Rather than find fault with their feelings or apologize for mine, I submit that time and experience can be a great shaper of opinion, as is evidenced by the dramatic increase in Americans traveling to Vietnam over the last few years. The experiences I had with the Vietnamese people, and the circumstances under which I grew to know them, caused me to admire, respect, and like a substantial number of them.

We typically celebrate victorious commanders and armies. But how should we judge those who fought bravely for the losing side? Should the unsuccessful outcome of the losers negate their accomplishments? For example, how should we evaluate Confederate ranger John S. Mosby? Mosby was successful but he ultimately could not forestall the final Union victory. This is also the case with the various U.S. supported programs in Vietnam. Some can be considered successful even though we lost the war. Although the North Vietnamese finally won the war, the amnesty program described in this book was successful. It saved many lives that may have otherwise been lost.

Insofar as I have failed to restrict the expression of my own opinions—political and otherwise—in this book, they are emphatically my own and do not represent those of any government agency or any organization.

Acknowledgements

I wish to express my deep gratitude to those Vietnamese and American friends who encouraged me to write this book, and to all those who, in sharing their lives, made the book possible. In particular, I am grateful to the late Ogden Williams, Bill Graham, and my wife, Barbara Carter-Garms, for the assistance they have all provided.

CHAPTER I

The Way to Dragon Land

It was the fall of 1966, and I had just returned to the United States after two years in India as a Peace Corps volunteer assigned to an agricultural development program. After completing that program, I spent the next two months at the University of Missouri helping to train a new group of volunteers bound for West Bengal, India.

The completion of the training project found me at a loss as to what to do next; I wasn't prepared yet to settle down to do graduate studies. Similarly, the thought of returning to southern Minnesota to take up farming with my father didn't sufficiently inspire me.

Obviously, I was going to have to find a job; I had worked my way through college, and my Peace Corps money had gone to pay off the last of the debts I had incurred in obtaining an education. Facing a bank account with zero was distressing, but was also a strong motivator.

For the time being, though, I decided to ignore all realities. A friend, Ken Goodmiller, and I took off in an old red Volkswagen to bum around on the West Coast. December

David J. Garms

1966 found us in Port Angeles, Washington. There, in a cheap motel, we took refuge from the snowy, wet weather.

I had been out of contact with my family for weeks. Acting on a combination of inspiration and guilt, I left our dingy room and went outside to a pay phone. A moment later, I learned from my mother that someone with AID had been trying to reach me from Washington, D.C. Having no idea where I was or how to contact me, my mother had not been able to tell me of this until my phone call. She gave me a number and told me the man had said to call back collect.

I looked out the glass door of the phone booth at the swirling snow. I remembered a time of year before when, in a small clay house instead of a phone booth, while gazing over fields of rice shimmering in the hot sun instead of snow banks, I had filled out an application for a position with the agency. Since then, the memory of that application had drifted from my memory.

I returned the call from Washington; a few moments later I was listening to the man offer me a job with the agency. My assignment would be Vietnam. Without hesitation, I accepted. The next day, I left my friend and Port Angeles behind, and got on a Greyhound bus traveling east.

It's often the case that people will make the most crucial decisions of their lives with less deliberation than they devote to everyday details. In my own defense, I could say that there were several halfway decent reasons to be on that eastbound bus. With zero in my bank account, I needed a job, and a stranger three thousand miles away had just offered me one.

A more sophomoric reason was that the job entailed spending several weeks in Washington for orientation, six months in Hawaii for Vietnamese language training and economic, political and cultural studies, and then eighteen months in Vietnam. I was a stranger to these places, and my experiences in India had done nothing to satiate my desire for

- 2 -

With the Dragon's Children

travel. I had never been to Vietnam, and whatever I might advocate regarding the future of their country, I had never met a single Vietnamese.

Another factor that influenced my thinking involved choice: I could either accept a position with AID in Vietnam or allow myself to be drafted. These reasons were sufficient to warrant serious consideration of the job, but they cannot explain my immediate acceptance of it. Perhaps I will never fully understand why I got on the bus. It could be that I was just another person whose reasons for making one of the most momentous decisions of his life would simply have to be laid to rest at the feet of inspiration.

During my weeks in Washington, I learned a good deal about AID and my place in the organization. I was told that in Vietnam I would work with one of the several U.S. sponsored programs for economic development, but that I would not know which of the programs I would be assigned to until I arrived in Saigon.

It was impressed upon me that I would be in Vietnam strictly as a non-combatant, and that I would not be required— nor should attempt on my own—to become directly involved in the war. Fortunately, no one tried to pretend that, by virtue of my very presence, I would not become thoroughly *indirectly* involved.

The next stop on the road from Port Angeles to Vietnam was a six-month training course in Hawaii. The training program was financed by AID and organized by the University of Hawaii. Thirty-six of us, with backgrounds ranging from business to teaching and from Peace Corps to military, arrived to take up residence in some abandoned Navy barracks in Ohana Nui, near Pearl Harbor. The last half of our training took place near Hilo on the big island of Hawaii. The primary purpose of the training was to give us a fair degree of fluency in the Vietnamese language. Additionally, we attended lectures

David J. Garms

on the history, culture, and economy of Vietnam, and carried out various research projects, both individually and in groups.

In Hawaii, halfway between my home and theirs, I finally met my first Vietnamese. Twelve of them had been hired to instruct us in the language. They were competent at their jobs, and invariably courteous and helpful. However, both formal instruction and informal contacts were carried out in a circumspect atmosphere. Some of the Vietnamese had military experience and some had not, but in all cases they avoided our questions on politics and the war.

From talking with them, it seemed almost as though the history of Vietnam had ended with the arrival of the twentieth century. They were far more practiced and agile in avoiding answers than we were in extracting them. I could not blame the Vietnamese, however, for the reluctance to communicate seemed to be less the result of deliberate deviousness than of deep, pervading weariness and sadness about the war in their country.

However, there was one interesting exception: Nguyen Van Duc, one of our language teachers—who was more talkative than the other teachers—wanted to learn how to drive a car and approached me and my friend, Tom Guilfoy, about this. We went with Mr. Duc to the Hawaii Department of Motor Vehicles (DMV) in the county capital of Hilo. Mr. Duc had with him his Vietnamese license to drive a motorcycle, but had no other documentation.

In a stroke of genius, Tom told the DMV clerk that Duc's permit was a driver's permit written in Gaelic and that he would be glad to translate it for her. Tom then glanced over to see how many lines there were on the Hawaii DMV form and provided the exact amount of information needed for a Hawaiian driver's permit. At this point, we had considerable trouble restraining our laughter, and left the DMV building as fast as we could.

With the Dragon's Children

Guilfoy claimed that he had done his job and that it was now time for me to teach Duc how to drive. I didn't realize how hard this was going to be. I had spent many hours with Duc in a car with an automatic transmission. Things weren't getting much better. One day I had really had it with Duc, and I said that if he didn't stop using his left foot on the brake and the right foot on the accelerator at the same time, I would cut his left leg off. He seemed to detect considerable seriousness on my part, and his driving skills improved dramatically after that.

My early attempts to understand the language were as frustrating as my attempt to understand the people. I had learned, to varying degrees, two of the languages of the Indian subcontinent, but I almost despaired of ever attaining even minimal fluency in Vietnamese. Vietnamese, like Chinese, is a tonal language. There are six different tones in Vietnamese, and every word in the language must be pronounced with one or another of the six tones. To use the wrong tone with the word would be equivalent to a foreign visitor in the United States saying "chip" for "ship," "ice" instead of "eyes," and "day" for "die." The difficulty in learning the tones and pronouncing them properly is compounded by the fact that, until the ear is trained (and partial hearing loss in my right ear didn't help), the subtle differences between tones cannot always be heard, much less repeated. It must have afforded our Vietnamese teachers with some much-needed amusement to witness our first attempts at speaking their language.

A teacher would stand before us and instruct us to repeat, "He's waiting by the bridge."

In unison we would say, "He's waiting by the toilet."

"The man ran fast," the teacher would continue.

A roomful of Americans would scream at him, "The man ran blood."

David J. Garms

When I confided my frustration to my teachers, they tried to reassure me by telling me that I would pick it all up quite easily once I was in Vietnam. I wasn't so sure.

While still in Hawaii, I had my first serious doubts about my decision to go to Vietnam. *What have I done?* I asked myself. My experiences in India had been pretty searing at times, but whatever I had encountered—including poverty and famine—it wasn't even in the same league with what might be ahead for a foreigner who stuck himself in the midst of another country's civil war.

Fortunately, the training program came to an end before I panicked completely. On a lovely blue Hawaiian morning in July of 1967, a group of us was taken to the airport to board the plane. I read the words stamped on my ticket: "Saigon." It was then, finally, that I started to think seriously about what I was doing.

Practically everyone entering Vietnam for the first time half expects to be shot at least once within an hour of his arrival—after all, it's a war zone, isn't it? The new arrival is quick to resent the comparative calm and unconcern of the old-timer and to take him for a show-off. But the old-timer has simply learned to live with the facts, one of the facts being that however bad things might seem, sometimes they just aren't that bad, even in Vietnam; even when they are, you must learn to live with them. In the midst of the most horrible and inhuman situations, people show a remarkable tendency to go on somehow, weaving back together the torn threads of their lives. Not much later I was to begin learning how extraordinarily skilled the people of Vietnam are at such weaving.

As we disembarked from the plane at the Saigon airport, a blast of hot air enveloped us and almost drove us back inside. I was luckier than some in the group; my previous years in Asia had fortified me against tropical weather. We walked

- 6 -

With the Dragon's Children

toward the terminal, our eyes taking in jeeps mounted with .50 caliber machine guns, fighter planes, and troop transports. My friend, Steve Spangler, and I started through the maze of customs together and managed to emerge without much difficulty. With our passports newly stamped "abroad on an official assignment for the United States government," we entered the main section of the terminal. There we were met by Norma, an attractive African-American lady from the personnel division (which is what it was called back then, rather than human resources) of the Office of Civil Operations Rural Development Support, mercifully and better known as CORDS. This organization was the umbrella for rural pacification and development in Vietnam. CORDS was represented in every province.

Norma piled us and our luggage into her car and drove us into the city. Spangler and I anxiously kept our eyes on the Vietnamese along the sides of the road and wondered which of them were Vietcong. We had our windows rolled up, despite the humidity and heat; after reading so many newspaper stories about terrorist activities in Saigon, we half expected grenades to come hurling toward us at any moment. We were amazed by Norma's total calm. While we were trying to concentrate on keeping an eye out for terrorists, she was pointing out the various sites along the road. Of course, Norma had been in Saigon awhile.

Norma drove us to an AID-leased hotel called The Excelsior. The hotel was on Nguyen Hue Street, one of Saigon's busiest. On one end of Nguyen Hue was the imposing City Hall. The bustling waterfront was at the other end. In between were numerous shops, hotels, bars and offices.

After we had checked into The Excelsior, Norma invited us over to her apartment for a drink. Feeling adrift our first day in Saigon, we were touched by her kindness and immediately accepted.

Night came while we were in her apartment, and with it our initiation into the war. We heard a thick, ominous thud somewhere in the distance. (I've always thought the sound rather resembled that of a bowling ball being dropped on a thick carpet.) Norma paused in the process of mixing another round of drinks and simply said, "A bomb—one of ours is being dropped somewhere outside the city. Happens every night, almost." A moment later, another bowling ball hit the carpet.

Later, as Spangler and I headed back to our hotel, the war appeared to be in full swing. There were sounds of artillery and the firing of weapons in the distance as well as bombs dropped from planes. With the night filled with the sounds of war, we wondered if we hadn't had too much to drink and were imagining things, because the streets were jammed with Vietnamese who appeared not to hear any of it. They were strolling nonchalantly along the sidewalks, weaving in and out of traffic on bicycles or motorcycles, and selling snacks from trays and carts along the curbs.

As many Americans before and after us have done, Spangler and I spent most of our first night in Saigon watching the war. We ascended to the roof of our hotel for a better view. Helicopters circled and fired at positions just beyond the city limits. Airplanes cut across the sky, dropping bombs. The explosions of the bombs and the burst of artillery rang in our heads. Smoke and fire could be seen from miles around and in every direction.

Early the next morning, I set out for a brief exploration of Saigon, anxious to see it without the sound effects of war in the background. Saigon is a mongrel city; once a lazy, shady colonial city of two hundred thousand, it has metamorphosed into a wartime capital of two million. It is a graceful city where anything is possible.

Despite the rush to plow through roads and push up buildings, there are still some touches left of Saigon's

With the Dragon's Children

once-famed greenery in the parks and the rows of trees along some of the streets. The city was designed by the French, as is evidenced by the boulevards, traffic circles, and many of the government buildings. Still, the Vietnamese preserved some of their own ways, which could be seen by the presence of open markets and the Buddhist temples that owed nothing to the west.

The history of Vietnam can be glimpsed in many of the signs over shops and buildings. Usually, the biggest letters are Vietnamese. Chinese characters are set just under the Vietnamese and are almost as large. In smaller letters, and closer to the bottom of the sign, is the French equivalent. Finally, at the very bottom of the sign, or sometimes on a separate sign altogether, the name of the shop or business is proclaimed in English. Some of Saigon's newest structures dispense with the first three and declare their intention solely in English: "Rose Bar," "The Key Hole Club," "Cheap Charlie's," and "The Happy Room."

The predominant characteristic about Saigon today is its traffic. Cars, buses, bicycles, pedestrians, jeeps, taxis, animal-pulled carts, motorcycles, trucks, three-wheeled motorized cabs, tanks, armored personnel carriers, and man-pushed carts all share the same roads. As might be surmised, they do not always do so amicably.

From six in the morning until midnight (the non-curfew hours), the streets are a blinding rush of movement, noise, and smoke. Traffic signals, where they exist, do little to organize the bedlam as most Vietnamese regard such devices as a mere suggestion.

Some of Saigon's typical vehicles are worthy of description. The most common variety of motorized taxi is an ancient, French-built Renault car. On a daily basis, drivers accomplish the most impressive feats just to keep the vehicles moving. Slowing down at corners or intersections is avoided at all costs

David J. Garms

in order to spare the driver—and the engine—the trouble of having to rev up all over again. When a stop is absolutely necessary, the driver begins pumping the brake at least half a block in advance. It is rare for a ride to be completed without the driver having to jump out and bang away at some part of the vehicle at least once. Amazingly, the banging always seems to right things, and the ride can be resumed.

The dangerous three-wheeled taxis are called cyclos. One or two foolhardy riders sit in the front of the open vehicle to serve as a human "bumper" while the driver controls things from a perch behind the passenger seat. The vehicle is without sides or roof, and as the two-cycle engine does not lend itself to precision control, these cyclos are among the most dangerous of Saigon's vehicles.

The drivers, a rough-and-ready lot, form quite a clique. They paint their chariots in a variety of wild colors and often stick flowers in their hats, giving a visitor the impression that they constitute Saigon's first "flower children." The drivers will hail each other from across the street and sometimes entertain their passengers, for no extra charge, with an impromptu drag race.

The bicycle rickshaw is the non-motorized version of the cyclo. The passengers sit in front while the driver pedals the vehicle from behind him. This is frightfully hard work for the drivers, and I was told that their health could not stand up for long. Typically, rickshaw drivers are peasants or refugees from North Vietnam who recently arrived in Saigon; they often cannot afford to begin work in the big city with a taxi or the motorized cyclo.

Finally, there is the Lambretta. With war making a regular bus system difficult, the Lambretta is the most common means of mass transportation. It's a small, three-wheeled vehicle, with the seat in front for a driver and two rows of benches in back for the passengers. The rear section

With the Dragon's Children

appears to hold approximately two and a half midgets, but as many as a dozen Vietnamese make use of it by squeezing into the seats, climbing up on the roof, and hanging onto the sides. Sometimes bags of produce and livestock may be tied to the side of the Lambretta. Since the vehicle has only three small wheels and is usually drastically overloaded, it is very unstable and is known to be one of the most accident-prone vehicles on the road.

On that first exploratory afternoon, still dizzy from my first look at Saigon, I joined Spangler and reported to the CORDS personnel office. Norma informed Spangler that he'd been assigned to NLD (the New Life Development Division), a program designed to assist with rural reconstruction. She wasn't certain about me, but she had heard that I might work with the Chieu Hoi Program in the Delta. I quickly rummaged through my memory and recalled that this was the amnesty program for Vietcong. She suggested that I go speak with Ogden Williams, chief advisor to the government of South Vietnam for the Chieu Hoi Program.

Shortly afterward, I was sitting in Ogden Williams' office. He impressed me as a shrewd and persuasive administrator. Yes, I had been assigned to his division. Mr. Williams was excited about the program and its potential contribution to ending the war.

"Money-wise, the program is relatively inexpensive," he explained. "It's costing the United States government thousands of dollars to kill one Vietcong, whereas it costs only about $300 to bring one in under the Chieu Hoi Program."

Ogden went on to say that he tried to select people with Peace Corps or similar experience for this program. "It is my feeling," he said, "and also that of others in this office, that ex-Peace Corps types with their overseas 'grass-roots' experience are better equipped to work with the Chieu Hoi Program. We feel you will do better, because this is basically a field operation having some of the same 'grass-roots' situations. I'm going to send you to IV Corps[1] to work for Major Dick Riddle. Riddle is an Australian officer detailed to our program as the Chieu Hoi advisor for IV Corps. He's got a difficult job because there are sixteen provinces in his region. Riddle will be in later this afternoon—why don't you come back at about sixteen-thirty hours (1630h is military time for 4:30 PM) and I'll introduce you to him?"

I returned promptly at 4:30 PM and was introduced to Major Riddle. He struck me as being a very aggressive army officer. He was extremely tall, overshadowing my own six feet by several inches, and had dark hair and a bushy mustache. He was decked out in a bush shirt, ascot, dark trousers, and Wellington boots. His movements were swift, his brogue heavily-accented, and he was quick and witty. When one of his frequent witticisms was detected, he himself would roar the most loudly of all, drowning out laughter of a lesser decibel. Major Riddle didn't seem too excited about having me come to Region IV to work for him, and I could understand why—I certainly wasn't any personality match for him.

Mr. Williams and Major Riddle agreed that I should depart for the Region IV capital of Can Tho on Wednesday of the following week. After I was in Can Tho, Major Riddle would select my specific assignment from among the sixteen provinces in that region.

Saturday arrived. I passed the next several days continuing my exploration of Saigon and digesting all the materials I could find on the Chieu Hoi Program. I already knew that Chieu Hoi (literally meaning "invitation to return") was the amnesty program for Vietcong. (Roughly, *Chieu* is pronounced the same as the English word *chew*, and *Hoi* rhymes with *toy*.) The program offered the Vietcong an alternative to being

With the Dragon's Children

captured as prisoners of war or killed. By voluntarily turning himself in, a Vietcong—after completing a re-indoctrination program of about two months at one of the Chieu Hoi Centers scattered throughout the country—would be reinstated into the good graces of the GVN. With modifications, the program was a carryover from the experiences of the government of the Philippines with the Huk insurgency of the early 1950s, and the British government in Malaysia with the terrorists in the 1960s.[2]

American advisers in South Vietnam developed and refined the program, and presented it to the government in 1963. When persuaded of the importance of taking manpower away from the Vietcong, the government of South Vietnam (GVN) accepted the program, though with some reluctance. Rudy Yabut, a captain in the Philippine Army, was one of the officials involved in persuading the Vietnamese government to design and implement the Chieu Hoi program nationwide. (Later, Rudy would be my regional supervisor in the delta.)

When Wednesday arrived, I boarded a C-47 aircraft (a cargo plane outfitted with seats along both sides of the aircraft) with Steve Spangler and another man who had also just been assigned to the New Life Development Division in the Delta. As the C-47 wound its way down into the heart of the Delta, I saw rice paddies, small clusters of houses, rivers and canals. What especially caught my attention were the bomb craters—there were so many of them that they appeared to have been sprinkled from a pepper shaker.

The plane landed at the Can Tho air base. My two companions were met by the Region IV chief of the NLD. As there was no one at the air base to meet me, I went over to the NLD chief and asked, "Have you seen Major Riddle around today?"

"No, why?" he responded.

"I've been assigned to the Chieu Hoi Program; a cable was sent ahead to announce my arrival time."

- 13 -

David J. Garms

"Those cables have a way of getting lost," he said. "Look, I'll drive you over to the CORDS headquarters with these guys and you can take it from there. The regional Chieu Hoi office is not too far away, and you can find a taxi."

We arrived at the CORDS regional headquarters, and I went on to get a taxi as suggested. I tried using a little Vietnamese on the driver and he responded enthusiastically, bombarding me with all sorts of questions:

"Where did you study Vietnamese? Who sent you to Vietnam? Do you have a wife?"

Chieu Hoi headquarters for Region IV was located in a rather dismal alley. Painstakingly, I translated the sign over the entrance: "Dai Dien Chieu Hoi Vung IV Chieu Thuat," into "Open Arms Representative for Region IV." As nonchalantly as possible, I entered the building, walked into the first office I saw, and introduced myself. It so happened that I had introduced myself to no less than the representative, Colonel Thuc. He was polite, but he had no idea what to do with me. As his English was about on a par with my Vietnamese, we conducted our conversation in a mixture of each, to the detriment of both.

Finally, Colonel Thuc ordered a clerk to see if anyone was in the office of the advisor just across the hall. The clerk returned with the deputy advisor, Rudy Yabut. After introductions, Captain Yabut took me back with him to the advisor's office. I mentioned that I had met Major Riddle in Saigon and that we'd agreed that I would come to Can Tho on this day. Captain Yabut apologized for the confusion and explained that Major Riddle had to spend most of his time on field inspections all over the Delta; he was expected back later in the afternoon.

Yabut briefed me on some of the aspects of the program. Major Riddle would assign me to be the province Chieu Hoi advisor of one of the sixteen provinces in the region. He also informed me that I would be the first American to hold this post in the Delta. The regional chief, Major Riddle, was, of

With the Dragon's Children

course, Australian. The provincial advisers under him at this time were Filipinos, some of whom had had personal experience in their own country with the counterinsurgency against the Huks. I felt at a distinct disadvantage; I knew nothing at all about the Chieu Hoi Program except for what I'd hurriedly digested in Saigon, and I certainly could boast no previous experience with counterinsurgency.

Major Riddle returned from his field trip that afternoon, but he seemed too preoccupied to talk with me about my assignment. I continued to stand around the office talking with different people. Captain Yabut continued to feed me tidbits on the program. I also began to read through files, pamphlets, and anything else I could find on the Chieu Hoi Program in the Delta. After several days of reading, talking with people, and reading some more, I began to feel somewhat more secure about my grasp of the program.

I also filled my time with walks around Can Tho. I was glad that I would not be working there. Can Tho, in the heart of the Delta, was a sprawling, depressing city. Even the main streets had ruts in them, and the buildings were shabby. The Mekong River ran right through the city, which was itself built over a swamp; the roads were muddy after even the lightest rain. If you kicked over a stone you would reach water level, and during the monsoon season, all the streets of the city were under water.

Unattractive though Can Tho was, it was certainly not unimportant; it was the primary economic convergence point of the Delta, and the Delta contained the most productive land in South Vietnam. By waterways and by roads, enormous amounts of produce were brought into Can Tho. Most of the produce was destined for Saigon.

Several days after I arrived in Can Tho, Major Riddle called me into his office and said that he had decided to send me to visit with some of the province advisors in the field. I

- 15 -

visited a total of four provinces and found the experience very enlightening. I was given a briefing by each of the province advisors, who were very friendly and knowledgeable.

It was evident, though, that these Filipino officers were being discriminated against by the U.S. advisory teams and were left out of the mainstream of provincial team activity and information. They resented it, but usually remained silent.[3] The Vietnamese on the staff were equally helpful. If I indicated the slightest interest in their work, they would make every effort to provide me with information.

I was shown around each of the Chieu Hoi Centers. There was a good deal of activity going on, but it was difficult to tell how effective it was simply by watching. Returnees came in, were re-indoctrinated and provided with vocational training, and then released.

As I observed the returnees going about their business at the centers, I found myself wondering just how converted they actually were. Could men really change sides quite so easily? I knew I would have to know these men very well before I could venture any opinions on their true feelings.

Valuable though the field trip had been, I was eager to return to Can Tho to learn if Major Riddle had decided what to do with me. When I returned from my travels, I soon discovered that he had indeed.

"I'm sending you to Go Cong because it's really screwed up!" he said. After allowing a moment for this to sink in, he continued. "It's a complete mess up there. The province chief of Go Cong is using the Chieu Hoi staff as his own little guerrilla band. The returnee rate has gone way down, and some returnees are re-defecting because living conditions at the center are so bad. Go to Go Cong and see if you can do something. I think I can get you on a Porter (a Swiss-made jet prop plane) aircraft tomorrow."[4]

- 16 -

With the Dragon's Children

My feelings regarding the assignment were very mixed. I appreciated that the job might be challenging, but I also resented being given an assignment that was known to be undesirable. I spent my last night in Can Tho building up the determination to do something with this "screwed-up" province.

CHAPTER II

A Town in the Delta

The trip to Go Cong was only a mere jaunt. (Roughly, *Go* rhymes with the English word *law*, and *Cong* is pronounced the same as *come*.) The Go Cong airstrip consisted of a widened section of the road that led from the province capital to a district town. For a plane to land, ground traffic had to be stopped at both ends of the widened section.

    The people were cooperative enough, but not the water buffalo. They continued to wander aimlessly along the road. The pilot swooped down and buzzed them, but this barely increased their wandering speed. The buffalo raised their massive heads as if to muse, *Goodness! Wonder what that noise could be.* Buffalo travel in only one gear—super slow—and there is virtually nothing they might encounter that would persuade them to experiment with another. (On rare occasions, however, buffalo do get angry—and when they do, watch out; I once observed an irate buffalo plowing through several thatched village houses.)

    When the buffalo had finally wandered off the strip of their own accord and the plane was about to land, a passenger

With the Dragon's Children

observed, "This is Go Cong International Airport, where Lambrettas try to take off at the same time that a plane lands." I could see from my window that Saigon's answer to mass transportation had been exported to the provinces—with a few added refinements: the inside of the three-wheeled vehicle was bursting with humanity, the top was heaped full of baskets of vegetables, and live ducks and chickens were tied in bunches along the sides. In some cases, piglets' feet had been strung together, and they too were hauled up to the top. It looked like a Noah's Ark on wheels, with all the sound effects.

I got off the plane, looking back all the time to see if the aircraft would be able to take off without running into a buffalo or a Lambretta. Romeo Raneses, the Chieu Hoi advisor of Go Cong, was waiting for me beside the road. He seemed relieved to receive his successor. He was also somewhat curious to see what an American would do with a job previously held by Filipinos.

As he drove me into town, Raneses explained that things were indeed very bad. The province chief had made killers out of the APT (Armed Propaganda Team) members attached to the Chieu Hoi staff and would deliberately send them into areas controlled by the Vietcong. The Chieu Hoi chief of Go Cong (Raneses's Vietnamese counterpart and the man whom it was his primary duty to advise) had just been fired by the province chief for having protested to the Ministry of Chieu Hoi in Saigon about his use of the APT as his private guerrilla band. The protest was suicidal, though certainly commendable. I learned somewhat later that the former Chieu Hoi chief had sent the letter of protest largely due to Raneses's persuasion, and that the letter had been jointly signed by them. (Not surprisingly, the Vietnamese deeply resented having a foreigner so openly involved in their internal political affairs.) Obviously, I was going to be in the midst of a tricky situation.

- 19 -

David J. Garms

I had learned something about the APT during my field trip to other provinces in the Delta. Each province had an APT, and each team was made up entirely of ex-Vietcong. The APT was supposed to be a political propaganda arm of the government in general and of the Chieu Hoi Program in particular. The members were to be armed only for the purpose of defending themselves in contested areas. They were supplied with the weapons of psychological warfare— bullhorns, public address systems, and leaflets for dissemination—to enable them to effectively convey the desired message.

As they were all former Vietcong themselves, it was thought that they could speak persuasively about their own reasons for defecting and about their "new life with the GVN." It was believed that such persons would reap great political and psychological benefits for the side that now claimed their loyalty. In practice, however, the toughest and fiercest of the returnees tended to join the APT, and their enthusiasm for killing their former comrades sometimes surpassed that for converting them. They could be a difficult lot to control; the province chief of Go Cong, rather than control them, had actually incited their violent tendencies.

Raneses drove me through narrow streets—bustling with pedestrians, pigs, and chickens—to the CORDS headquarters in the center of the town. I was assigned living quarters in the compound and told that I could take my meals at the mess in the MACV (Military Assistance Command Vietnam) compound. Feeling stripped of my status as a civilian, I was introduced to members of the U.S. Provincial Advisory Team. I was quite relieved to see that many of them were civilians too, but by now I had begun to realize that in Vietnam the line between civilian and military was blurred.

Raneses next suggested that we go immediately to inspect the Go Cong Chieu Hoi Center situated just outside the town.[5] At a glance I could see that no one had exaggerated

With the Dragon's Children

about how bad it was. The buildings were inadequate and badly run down. There was no latrine and almost no provisions for the returnees' recreation or vocational training. The perimeter barrier was very poor; if the center was attacked it could be overrun with ridiculous ease.

The morale of the Chieu Hoi staff was terrible. Many of them had stopped coming to work because they viewed the situation as being devoid of hope. Not having received their salaries in months didn't help matters. The number of arrivals at the center had been decreasing while the number of re-defections was increasing.

Difficulties were compounded by the fact that no new Chieu Hoi chief had been appointed. Whoever it would be, I feared that I, his advisor, would be of little help to him at first. The deputy Chieu Hoi chief, acting chief in the interim, was not likely to be valuable in assisting either of us to learn our new jobs. He was so lacking in courage and integrity that he was unable to bring himself to request from the province chief the withheld payment of staff salaries which had already been budgeted for and approved by Saigon. (However, I probably would have found less fault with him had I known the province chief at the time.)

As I walked around the Chieu Hoi Center, I became very upset. How could anyone permit human beings to live in this condition, much less human beings whose loyalty was being courted? There were no mosquito nets and no blankets in the sleeping quarters. The buildings (two for returnee living quarters and one each for food preparation, administration, and lectures) were not separated by hard surfaced paths. It was already the rainy season, and it was impossible to take a step without having mud half-way up to the knee. Since there was no latrine, the returnees simply used the sides of the buildings. The determination that had developed after I learned of my assignment was fast dissolving, becoming as soggy as the mud around my feet.

Fortunately, I did not have to spend my first evening in Go Cong pursuing my depressing thoughts. I was invited to the home of a Go Cong resident, Le Ngoc Diep, for a combination farewell party for Raneses and welcome party for me. (Diep's official position was that of district Chieu Hoi chief of Hoa Tan, one of Go Cong's four districts, but he spent most of his time at the provincial center where his skills in administration and maintenance were badly needed.)

Diep's home was perched on the side of a little hill next to the river. About twenty-five guests were present. Each table (on which a plastic tablecloth had been placed) seated about four guests; rice bowls were turned upside down to keep out the dust, and chopsticks were placed on top of carefully-folded paper napkins. I was impressed with the meticulousness of the arrangements.

Our host, Mr. Diep, invited us to sit down. The jumbo-sized drinking glasses were upturned and filled with large chunks of ice, and large bottles of Larue beer were brought out.[6] Several dogs were wandering about the room; we could hear chickens and pigs in pens next to the house; ducks quacked in the river nearby.

Our first course—crab—was brought to the tables, and we all tore at the shells in search of the morsels of meat. I was placing my picked-over crab shells on the table, but I saw that the rest of the guests were throwing theirs on the floor. The dogs were running between and under the tables to scoop them up. "Throw your shells on the floor, too," I was advised. "When the party is over, that's where they'll end up anyway."

I did as I was instructed, and discovered that it was fun to toss the shells over my shoulder and hear the *clunk* as they hit the floor. Dinner continued, and the consumption of beer and food increased. The noise of crab shells—and later,

- 22 -

With the Dragon's Children

chicken and duck bones—hitting the floor increased, as did the laughter. The party was going well.

The women were back in the kitchen preparing the food. They did not take part in the party, and could only be seen occasionally peeking around the corner to check on the "progress." A number of children were running around the tables or playing outside, but they did not eat with the men either.

The guests seated with me began to ask me questions in Vietnamese:

"Do you have a wife?"

"Do you like Vietnamese women?"

"How old are you?"

"Do you like Vietnamese food?"

"How long will you stay in Go Cong?"

The questions tended to be specific, so I was able to answer most of them. Soon I responded with a few questions of my own:

"How old are you?"

"How many children do you have?"

"What do you think of Americans?"

We were all drinking a lot of beer and enjoying ourselves immensely. The Vietnamese at my table had learned my name and were calling me "Ong Gam" ("Mr. Garms").[7] One Vietnamese at the table was particularly impressed by my small degree of fluency. He remarked that few Americans in Vietnam took the time or were able to learn the language, and that there was only one other American, of the 90 in the province, with whom he could carry on a conversation. That person was Jim Collins, the provincial Joint U.S. Public Affairs Office (JUSPAO) representative. He grew more and more ecstatic over my feeble efforts. Finally, he stood up, pointed at me, and screamed to the rest of the room, "This American speaks Vietnamese!" Immediately I was surrounded by Vietnamese trying to put questions to me all at once.

- 23 -

David J. Garms

At the same party, I was asked one surprising question: "Why do Americans smell?"

Of course, we all smell different, depending on what we eat and how we groom ourselves. Nevertheless, I was totally unprepared for such a question, but I was pleased to see that the comfort level with my colleagues—facilitated by the beer intake—was at the point where they would ask almost anything, even if it was embarrassing. After a long pause on my part, I decided to ask for specifics. I was advised that there was some unique smell that Americans had and that American men use fragrances that should only be used by women. As far as I could determine, the fragrances referred to were after-shave colognes.

The party had some repercussions. Within a few days, word got around the province:

"There is this new American—and he can speak Vietnamese!"

People would go out of their way to approach me to learn if the story was true; they were awed by and delighted with the slightest response that I might give. I began to feel like a newly-discovered talking dog. I could scarcely believe the excitement over such a small thing, but then, Go Cong was one of the few places in Vietnam where simply being an American was a novelty.

The lady secretaries at the Chieu Hoi Center developed a peculiar reaction to my ability to speak some Vietnamese. Every morning, the moment I walked into the office, one of them would approach me and ask some simple question. She would then repeat my answer to another lady, and they would both begin to giggle. The answer would be repeated to each of the secretaries in turn until the entire office was in an uproar. Their reaction would be the same, even when I happened to

With the Dragon's Children

give a perfect response to the question. I couldn't resent their laughter as it helped the staff begin the day in a good frame of mind.

Significant improvements at the center could not begin at once, due to the absence of a Chieu Hoi chief and my own unfamiliarity with the situation, but I was already committed to remaining. Go Cong might have lacked some of the facilities of Can Tho or Saigon (now called Ho Chi Minh City), but in every important way it was a definite improvement. My attachment to the province was growing fast.

The people of Go Cong were pleased to tell me the history of their province, though as a separate province it had existed only since 1963.[8] In that year, the Saigon government had decreed that Dinh Tuong province was too big for effective administration. The coastal portion of the original province was given the name of its largest town, Go Cong. The name of the province and the name of its capital were, therefore, the same.

The people of Go Cong (or, as they called themselves, "Nguoi Go Cong") were pleased with the split; it provided them with a more accessible provincial government; they had more opportunities to enter the lower ranks of the provincial bureaucracy, although all senior officials continued to be appointed by Saigon.

Most of these senior officials were not from Go Cong and therefore were not familiar with the local people or their customs. Their loyalties were firmly affixed to Saigon. In some cases, however, these "foreigners" grew to appreciate Go Cong and adopted the interests of its people as their own. When this became too evident to Saigon, the usual result was that the official would be removed from Go Cong and sent off to be a "foreigner" in another province. The people of Go Cong were often sad to see such a person leave them, but they would soon turn their attention to the "conversion" of a successor.

- 25 -

David J. Garms

In 1967, the province had a total population of about 181,000, of which approximately 24,000 resided in or near the capital. The remainder of the population was divided among Go Cong's four districts: Hoa Tan (45,000); Hoa Dong (45,000); Hoa Lac (37,000); and Hoa Binh (30,000).[9]

Go Cong's coastline stretches down the entire length of the province. Kien Hoa, the province just south of Go Cong, is largely forested with mangrove trees, and these forests have traditionally been strongholds of the Vietcong. The northern part of the forests extends into the southern areas of Go Cong.

The remainder of the province consists mostly of flat, very sparsely-forested farm land. Elevation throughout the province varies no more than a few feet above sea level, except where man has intervened. Dirt dikes are built up around the rice paddies to retain water, and the roads are built still higher to keep them above water level during the rainy season.

The most frequented sections of the roads are surfaced with asphalt laid over rock bedding. Many of the roads, however, are simply dirt. The numerous holes, ruts, and stones make cautious driving a necessity. (Nevertheless, some Americans traveled these roads at great speed, thinking that they could travel faster than a bullet from an AK-47.)

The province is interwoven with canals and the tributaries of many small rivers. Even the smallest hamlet can usually boast a fish pond. A river passes to the south of the town of Go Cong, and there is always considerable activity along its waterfront. Boats travel up and down the river transporting fish, vegetables, fruits, coconuts, and livestock to the markets.

These boats are given distinctive touches by their owners. Faces are painted in bright colors on the prow, often with special attention given to the eyes and teeth. Most faces are intended to inspire fear and respect. The dragon is the most common motif; throughout their more than two thousand

- 26 -

With the Dragon's Children

years of history, the dragon has been an object of particular good fortune and reverence to the Vietnamese people.

Livestock is an important industry in Go Cong. Pigs, ducks, and chickens run loose everywhere. A few families confine their poultry to pens and tie their pigs to stakes. (One method of firmly fixing a pig to a stake was to pierce an ear, insert a piece of rope through the ear, and tie the rope to a stake.) The people of Go Cong seem to have a special fondness for pigs, and almost every family will be raising at least one or two at all times. The people seem simply to enjoy having them around, but they also like the profit that can almost always be realized when the pigs are shipped to Saigon.

Buffalo are common in the countryside. When not being used for plowing the rice paddies, the buffalo pass the time roaming around, seemingly oblivious to their surroundings. Usually a small boy will be watching over a herd of buffalo. He walks beside them, trying to direct their movements with a stick that is longer than him. Often the little boy will tire of trying to control the aimless monsters and will climb up on the back of one of them and enjoy a ride while the animals roam where they wish.

Ducks are as ubiquitous as chickens and pigs. It is a common sight to see a young boy or an elderly man watching over a flock of ducks, numbering anywhere from one hundred to three hundred, as they scavenge for tiny fish and insects in the rice paddies.

The town of Go Cong has three very attractive Buddhist pagodas, one Catholic Church, and one Protestant church. The province is more than eighty percent Buddhist. Unlike other provinces in Vietnam, Go Cong has never experienced conflicts among the Buddhists, Catholics and Protestants. The Catholic Church, despite its small congregation, has the largest structure in the entire province. Its steeple soars above the rest of the countryside and can be seen from a vehicle or plane at a

- 27 -

David J. Garms

considerable distance. A French Catholic priest was in residence at the church; in an effort to appear neutral when the "Vietcong come to town," he stayed away from the Americans.

Most of the homes and other structures in the capital town are handsomely and sturdily constructed. The residents build either with wood or with brick and cement. The doors, windows, and supporting frames are often painted in bright red, green, or blue. Even the poorer people have homes, usually a thatched hut on the outskirts of the town. There are some tall trees and low shrubs along the sides of the streets. Many of the residents plant flowers beside their homes. Except in the outskirts, most of the streets are paved and are kept fairly clean—a surprising achievement in view of the difficulties faced due to the war.

The people of Go Cong are fortunate in their surroundings. The soil is fertile and the waters abundant with marine life. There is plenty of food available at prices lower than those in Saigon. There is little pressure on the land, and a job can be found for anyone who wants one. The people of Go Cong are able to lead a life denied to many of their countrymen by the differing circumstances of the environment. They tend to enjoy a relaxed lifestyle and are renowned for their social life. The town of Go Cong is often referred to by other Vietnamese (justly, in my opinion) as the "Drinking Capital of Vietnam."

It is hard not to think that Go Cong's relative well-being and contentment in the midst of war stemmed partially from its having been spared a major American presence, for there were no U.S. combat units stationed anywhere in the province. Occasionally the U.S. 9th Infantry Division troops stationed in neighboring Dinh Tuong Province would sweep through Go Cong in the pursuit of Vietcong units, but otherwise the defense of the province rested with the Vietnamese. The Americans in Go Cong, who numbered a total of about ninety in 1967, were, for the most part, limited to strictly advisory

With the Dragon's Children

roles. Those U.S. military personnel present advised the provincial military officers. All of them were housed in the MACV compound. U.S. civilians acted as advisors to the various public service offices such as health, police, agriculture, rural development and – with my arrival – Chieu Hoi. The civilians were assigned to comfortable prefabricated housing in the CORDS compound. Provisions for eating for both military and civilian personnel were in the MACV compound, where an army sergeant presided over the mess. The food at the mess was excellent; the Army sergeant in charge of the mess had an amazing skill; he could make anything taste good.

The people of Go Cong, like most Vietnamese, were not predisposed toward great admiration of or respect for the American character and manner. They thought us to be, on the whole, a loud-mouthed, clumsy, insensitive lot, lacking in dignity and manners. In their eyes, the honesty we so pride ourselves was viewed as either naïveté or ruthlessness. Our prized ability to get things done was interpreted as unmitigated aggressiveness or rampant discontent with everything in general. The Vietnamese view was that "some decisions take time." Unlike Vietnamese elsewhere, however, the people of Go Cong were prepared to at least *not dislike* Americans. Having escaped the presence of hordes of foreigners in their midst, they were willing to judge an American as an individual. An American who exhibited the slightest degree of interest in and respect for the way of life in Go Cong was likely to be stunned by the response. If he asked questions rather than bestowing advice like confetti, and if he conducted himself more in the manner of a guest than that of a host, there was virtually no facet of the local life into which he would not be welcomed.

In Saigon that first night, the war had seemed very close. I had expected it to seem still closer once I arrived in the Delta. Having the most fertile agricultural land in all South

- 29 -

David J. Garms

Vietnam, the Delta had naturally been heavily contested for many years by the GVN and the Vietcong. I was not mistaken in my expectations. In Go Cong I soon grew accustomed to hearing the 105-millimeter and the 155-millimeter howitzer shells virtually every night, and to the frequent sound of weapons being fired in the distance.

Artillery explosions would sometimes shake the buildings in town and cause glass in the windows to tinkle and clatter. Overhead, aircraft on bomb runs and helicopter gunships were common sights. Occasionally, when a fierce battle was taking place with the Vietcong, the "buffalo" would be brought out. (The "buffalo" was a C-47 aircraft outfitted with .50 caliber machine guns on both sides of the plane. When all the plane's machine guns were firing, it sounded like a buffalo experiencing great pain.)

People are capable of learning to adjust to almost anything—even the sounds and fears inherent with war. After the town had been heavily mortared during the night, people would go about their business as usual the following morning. Everywhere I looked, the people of Go Cong were managing to go on with their lives; I could scarcely fail to follow their example. I, too, learned to continue whatever I was doing—working, eating, talking, sleeping—with little regard for the sounds of war. I think I almost learned not to even hear them, except for incoming mortars and rockets. In any case, until Tet of 1968, no actual combat took place inside the town boundaries. However close the war might sound, it was at least a mile or two away.

During the day, it was possible for even an American, with minimal security precautions, to travel in relative safety to the district villages of Go Cong—but the night was always different. In the smaller hamlets, the coming of the night brought the ascendancy of the "other government of South Vietnam." The peasants' plaintive assertion that they were

- 30 -

With the Dragon's Children

caught between GVN rule by day and Vietcong rule by night had in it more than a little truth. Several hamlets had both the GVN and Vietcong flags and would hoist the right flag at the appropriate time.

Under the guidance of Raneses—who remained in Go Cong for two weeks after my arrival—and other members of the staff, I gradually began to understand my duties as the Chieu Hoi advisor for Go Cong. Officially, my primary duty was to act as advisor to the Chieu Hoi chief on all matters relating to the program. In my case as in Raneses', the major concern was with the returnees themselves. This concern ran the gamut from the employment of inducement themes to encourage their leaving the Vietcong, to their final reemployment as citizens in good standing. In between were such matters as their reception at the center, compensation for weapons they brought in, their billeting and feeding, exploiting them for intelligence purposes, their political re-indoctrination, and their vocational training.

I was also to turn my attention to advising the Chieu Hoi chief on the proper use of the staff, including the APT. Another of my primary responsibilities was to assist with the preparation of the Chieu Hoi budget and to monitor the expenditure of GVN and U.S. monies for the program. Finally, I was to serve as liaison officer to the province senior advisor and the regional Chieu Hoi advisor in Can Tho (Major Riddle) on all matters pertaining to the Chieu Hoi Program in Go Cong Province. Another role for me that evolved over time was to review intelligence information collected from the Vietcong returnees and pass it to the Military Assistance Command – Vietnam (MACV).[10]

The position, as I quickly realized, was deceptive. My responsibilities were far-reaching, but my actual authority was virtually non-existent. Real power rested with the Chieu Hoi chief, and however thoroughly and constantly I might

David J. Garms

advise him, I had no intrinsic authority to compel him to heed my advice in the slightest degree. Complaining of his intransigence to his Vietnamese superiors, such as the province chief, was likely to be of no avail as he had probably received his appointment largely through their support. Even if his superiors might agree with my case, they were not in the habit of viewing sympathetically an American's complaint with the way in which a fellow Vietnamese performed his duties.

Taking my complaints to my own American superiors would be even less fruitful as they too were advisors and had no more real power to command the obedience of a Vietnamese official than I had. It would result in just another all-too-common case of a group of Americans sitting around complaining of the unwillingness of the Vietnamese to follow their advice.

Obviously, then, my effectiveness in my job would largely be determined by the nature of the personal relationship that I managed to achieve with my counterpart. If I could gain his respect and trust, and perhaps even his friendship, then he might well permit me to carry out my responsibility as his advisor. In any case, I was fully aware that I would advise solely at his pleasure.

My position was not only potentially unworkable, it was also, in its very essence, more than slightly ridiculous. I could imagine what might prevail in the minds of a people far less sensitive than the Vietnamese at the presence in their midst of a twenty-four-year-old foreigner who could claim only a few years' experience of any kind—and none at all in their country, but who, nevertheless, was among them for the purpose of advising them on the conduct of their internal affairs.

In addition, it was evident to me—and must have been equally so to the Vietnamese—that regardless of whether my advice might prove wise or not, and whether it was heeded or not, I would leave them one day and would never have to face the consequences of what I had done. For me, this time among

With the Dragon's Children

them accounted for a limited number of todays, and when tomorrow arrived, I would be going home. For the Vietnamese, no tomorrow could entirely escape the consequences of today. They *were* home.

I had some time to learn my responsibilities and to ponder the strangeness of my situation before the arrival of the Chieu Hoi chief. As no one had informed me who it would be or when he could be expected, the arrival itself came as a total surprise.

One morning I walked into my office and there he was: a handsome man considerably taller and huskier than most Vietnamese. His well-starched uniform, polished boots, and erect bearing signified a professional soldier. In his calm, smiling face I read somewhat more—the character of an intelligent, decisive, and sensitive person. This was Lieutenant Nguyen Van Trieu, and though I didn't know it yet, he would become my friend.

The entrance of Lieutenant Trieu (pronounced *tree-oh*) also marked my real introduction into certain aspects of politics in Vietnam. I was aware that the Ministry of Chieu Hoi in Saigon had been displeased with the province chief's peremptory dismissal of the previous Chieu Hoi chief. I had seen the cable from the ministry stating, "We deeply regret to inform you that the Ministry of Chieu Hoi has no replacement to send to Go Cong at this time. Will advise later." I had interpreted this as meaning simply that, for reasons known only to themselves, the people in the ministry were not going to appoint a new chief for our center at this time.

However, the cable had special significance for the province chief. He interpreted it as representing strong criticism of his dismissal of the previous Chieu Hoi chief. Originally, he might not have cared whether the center ever had a new chief or not, but his feeling that he had been criticized and insulted galvanized him into action. He reasserted himself by suddenly appointing Lieutenant Trieu as acting Chieu Hoi chief.

The appointment of a permanent chief could, as he well knew, be accomplished only by the ministry, but with this move he had succeeded in his intention to return an insult. Now it was his turn to indirectly accuse the ministry of not looking after the interests of the Chieu Hoi Program in Go Cong. The game was not over, and we would all eventually have to cope with the ministry's retaliation, but for the time being, the province chief had succeeded in effectively conveying the message that he would do as he pleased in his own province.

Though a province chief (the equivalent of a United States state governor) is paramount in his province, he himself is appointed by Saigon. Officially, he is appointed by the Ministry of the Interior in coordination with the Ministry of Defense. This is also true at the next level down, that of the district chiefs.[11]

In the selection of both province and district chiefs, however, the president of the country largely plays a passive role. The province chief of Go Cong held the rank of colonel in the ARVN (Army of the Republic of Vietnam), but this was not remarkable as, at this time, all province and district chiefs were military officers. Because a province chief usually owed his position to Saigon rather than to the people he was to lead—as well as having military training rather than political expertise, and an unlikelihood of being native to the province of which he was chief—he could very well have little sympathy for the people under his jurisdiction.

The province was his world, his empire. He was authorization officer for funds, moving supplies, changes in personnel, and most promotions. He could move troops at will anywhere in his province. This leaves a number of doors wide open for a province chief; he has sufficient latitude to achieve rapid

- 34 -

With the Dragon's Children

constructive development, or to reach heights of extortion and corruption.

Unfortunately, Colonel Tu, the Go Cong province chief, decided to go down the road of corruption. And Tu had plenty of experience in all matters related to corruption. He had been transferred from Dinh Tuong province to Go Cong because of corruption charges he faced in Dinh Tuong. Saigon, rather than hold him accountable, transferred Tu to Go Cong.[12]

The province chief of Go Cong had decided to appoint his own acting Chieu Hoi chief for personal political reasons. His choice of Trieu for the job was well thought through beforehand, and was also essentially political. First, the fact that Trieu was still a soldier put him under the direct command of a province chief who was a colonel. Second, Trieu came from Go Cong; he had no contacts with or loyalties to Saigon, and was, therefore, not at all likely to take up his difficulties with the ministry as his predecessor had done.

Oddly enough, despite all the circumstances of the appointment, the needs of the province chief and the needs of the Chieu Hoi Program converged in the person of Trieu. He was not a dreamer of the impossible, but a master of realizing the improbable. He managed to be loyal to the province chief without ever compromising his loyalty to his native province or his own morality. Trieu had a most difficult role to play, but he played it superbly—though his background would not have suggested as much.

He had been born in the northern part of Go Cong Province thirty-three years before. His peasant father died when Trieu was seven, leaving his small son to begin a life of menial labor at an early age. Trieu managed to go to school, and quickly proved to be a brilliant student; he received the assistance of his relatives and teachers and was able to go all the way through high school. Anything more was an impossibility, however, and so Trieu, like many other able but poor

- 35 -

David J. Garms

young Vietnamese, turned to the military for a career. He had been in the military ever since.

As he belonged to the regional army rather than to the national army, he had been stationed in his home province for almost all of that time. Trieu was a dedicated family man, already the proud father of five children when I first met him. As a lieutenant, he received about 10,000 pilasters a month.[13] To supplement his income, his wife, a cheerful, industrious woman, raised livestock in the backyard of their home and started a beer and soda distribution business. Trieu was proud of his wife and would comment to people that she had become an excellent business woman. Actually, the family would have fared badly without the additional income.

A man of Trieu's intelligence and initiative could easily have uncovered numerous other sources of income. He was an honest man, and he did not seem to care that in this he stood virtually alone. I didn't realize the full significance of this trait of his until I had been in Vietnam awhile; a number of Vietnamese had commented to me in wonderment that this man was totally incorruptible, and that the most "innocent" bribe was totally beyond him.

That first morning after his arrival at the office, Trieu and I talked of the situation at the center. As he spoke excellent English, we conducted our conversation in that language. Trieu said, "The people previously in charge here did not know how to love people to let them live in such a terrible condition. First, we must build a latrine. Then we're going to get blankets and mosquito nets for the returnees." I was impressed with his decisiveness and his concern.

Trieu did get the latrine, the blankets, and the mosquito nets. The latrine was placed on a platform in the middle of a fish pond with a wood walkway to it. The fish scooped up the human waste. Trieu also persuaded the province chief, who had suddenly become more cooperative than before, to give the

With the Dragon's Children

center some wheat, cooking oil, and cement from the provincial warehouse. Groups of returnees were already at work cleaning up the center. Trieu quickly brought the fractious APT to heel, and they resumed their efforts to persuade the Vietcong with propaganda instead of guns. The regular staff members who had not been bothering to show up for work suddenly displayed an amazing proclivity for industry, particularly after Trieu managed to extricate their back pay from the province chief.

Trieu and I quickly slipped into an easy partnership. We agreed on almost everything and had no real differences. We both believed in working hard because, as Trieu liked to say, "It makes you feel good at the end of the day." We also agreed that it was important to play hard, and we did our share of that, too. Somehow, the relationship between Trieu and me escaped falling victim to the whims of politics.

CHAPTER III

The Men Who Changed Sides

By the time Trieu arrived, I had begun to know the returnees at the center. I had been more than slightly apprehensive at first about working with them. After all, a matter of weeks or sometimes even days before, these men had been active Vietcong. Some of them had been fighting for years and had more than a few kills to their credit. Americans had been their particular enemies. The prospect of being surrounded daily by the returnees, and on occasions when no other staff members were present, unnerved me initially. I had expected to adjust to this somewhat unnatural situation, and I did. What I had not anticipated was that the situation would soon not strike me as at all unnatural, and that I would develop genuinely warm feelings for them as a group and as individuals.

My apprehension quickly faded when I realized that the returnees were as afraid of me as I was of them. At first I couldn't understand their obvious nervousness whenever I approached them. Though I was certainly bigger than most of them, I too was unarmed, and they vastly outnumbered me. A few halting conversations with them led me to the conclusion

With the Dragon's Children

that they genuinely feared that I might harm them. I began to realize that a large part of the propaganda with which they had been barraged had been directed against Americans. For so long they had thought of Americans as killers, rapists, and torturers. These images could not be easily erased. They had been fighting Americans for years, but I was the first American some of them had ever known.

Gradually, as they gained confidence in themselves and in me, the images we had had of each other faded, and mutual trust and interest took their place. Once some of the returnees began to talk to me, it became almost impossible to get them to stop. They would jabber endlessly about their feelings, ideas, and experiences. My growing facility with their language made it easier for them. They freely enlightened me about even their most violent experiences—assassinations, booby traps, burning villages, and torture—seemingly with no qualms at all. I encouraged them to talk. I wanted desperately to learn all I could about the Vietcong, and as I was not likely to know any active members, the next best thing was to know men who had once been Vietcong.

The majority of the returnees, as I soon discovered, had always been peasants.[14] They had been born and raised in villages so small that even the capital of Go Cong appeared to them as a major metropolis. Most of them had received very little education and were singularly lacking in any real political orientation. They were likely to accept anything they were told, but whether they were able to comprehend or believe it was often a different matter. The returnee with deep convictions and an appreciation for the subtleties of politics did exist, but he was the exception.[15] I came to the conclusion that most of them had become Vietcong because of circumstances virtually beyond their control, and that it had been other circumstances beyond their control that had brought them to the center. They were like pawns in a game—they could not see the faces of the players who moved them or understand the nature of the game itself.

The returnees did, however, know one thing about the game: it was dangerous and they were the ones primarily in danger. Most had become returnees at least partially because of their fear of being captured or killed. For the time being, at least, they had decided they would be relatively safer on the GVN side. If the circumstances should change, they were likely to change with them. The premium was on adaptability rather than steadfastness.

The possibility of infiltrators among the returnees in the center was a constant concern of the staff. Those who were identified in Go Cong and other provinces had usually been sent there to bring about the destruction of the center. In one such case in another province, the fake returnee, impressed by his reception and weary of fighting, confessed the plot and became a real returnee. In a similar case, a woman informed a startled Chieu Hoi chief that she had been sent to the center to seduce and obtain information from him. I heard of at least two cases where bombs were placed in centers by infiltrators.

Despite such examples, infiltration never seemed to have taken place on a significant scale. All returnees were fingerprinted, photographed, and had their records filed with the police. As the effectiveness of an agent largely depended upon his having no known association with the Vietcong, and as a returnee's past was always known, it was more likely that infiltration of the Chieu Hoi Program would take place on the staff level.

Furthermore, the returnees were expected to supply verifiable information about their Vietcong units. As an agent would have to withhold such information, this would place him under immediate suspicion. An agent was as great a threat to real returnees as he was to anyone else; realizing this, the

With the Dragon's Children

returnees tended to be anxious to uncover and report any such "Trojan horse" in their midst.

The Vietcong themselves, masters though they were at the art of placing agents, appeared to recognize the handicaps involved in the use of the returnees for their purposes, and generally avoided using them. During the thirteen months I was in Go Cong, only two infiltrators were uncovered among the one thousand returnees who passed through the center. As happens in most such cases, the two men were turned over to the national police and their status changed to that of prisoners of war.

Once I had gotten over my concern with infiltrators, I began to trust the returnees increasingly. I traveled everywhere in the province with them and went with them into their homes when they visited their families. I trusted them for some reasons I couldn't explain except that, once I knew them and liked them, it followed almost naturally that I must trust them as well.

I kept a carbine rifle at home for self-defense in the event of a night attack on the town, and when I traveled into the districts, Trieu would usually send an armed bodyguard along with me, but I didn't carry a weapon myself until Tet of 1968. Though the returnees could have found numerous opportunities to do me harm, my trust in them proved not to have been misplaced. I was probably safer in Go Cong, where I was known, than in any place else in Vietnam.

My trust in the returnees became so strong that I once did something rather foolish. A Vietcong returnee had been after me for awhile to visit an "opium den" in Hoa Dong district. I finally agreed to go see the den. We traveled on his motorcycle. After we entered the opium den I noticed two old men so totally out of it that they didn't notice our entrance. My friend

- 41 -

David J. Garms

started pressuring me to smoke the opium pipe. I declined and he didn't continue to pressure me.

A Vietcong could theoretically become a *hoi chanh* (returnee) by turning himself over to virtually any Vietnamese connected with the military or government or to any member of the Allied Forces. In the majority of cases, however, the would-be returnee went through a hamlet chief. Typically, a private citizen would approach the chief and inform him that he "happened" to know of a Vietcong who wanted to turn himself in. A time and a place would be negotiated. The chief would contact the district Chieu Hoi chief and inform him of the negotiations. The Vietcong, provided he had not changed his mind or lost his nerve in the meantime, would turn himself over at the assigned time and place. The district Chieu Hoi chief would then take him to the center, and he would be entered into the rolls as a returnee.

United States troops were also authorized to receive returnees; they were continually exhorted by their commanders and by broadcasts over Armed Forces Radio to remember that, once a Vietcong had approached them and declared his desire to become a returnee, he could not be treated as an enemy. Few such Vietcong elected to turn themselves over to Americans. They preferred—understandably so—to surrender to another Vietnamese.

Many new returnees were obviously terrified about the possible reception that awaited them. They had been promised amnesty and no retribution of any kind, but they could not be certain that the promises would be kept. It required more than a little courage for a man to decide to change sides and give up to an "enemy" whom he may have been fighting for years. Once he had done so, what new horrors might lie ahead? Doubtful though the returnees may have been initially, I was not aware of any cases where these particular promises were not kept.

With the Dragon's Children

No promises were made to the prisoner of war at all, and his situation differed drastically. It was often a tragic fact that any line could be drawn between the man who became a prisoner of war and one who became a returnee would have to be a very thin one indeed. This was particularly true in the case of a Vietcong who had become one at gunpoint. He might have wanted from the start of his association with the Vietcong to become a returnee, but the watchfulness of his comrades or his lack of knowledge of how to turn himself in prevented him from taking action immediately. Then it might be too late, and he might be captured and thrown into a prisoner of war camp to languish there interminably. Though he might never have been a Vietcong willingly, and might have been even that for only a matter of days, circumstances could make him a prisoner of war.

All the returnees were interviewed by an S-2 officer (province level intelligence). A Sergeant Ba was responsible for this task. The findings emanating from the interview were typed on a standard S-2 form. The returnees often provided valuable intelligence regarding Vietcong units, their location and future plans. This information was passed on to the provincial CIA officer and others as appropriate.

The GVN, recognizing the possibility of some Vietcong being less "guilty" than others, established a program which permitted special consideration to be accorded in such cases.[16] A prisoner of war was allowed to petition the prison warden and appeal to have his status changed to that of a returnee. The warden, after reviewing the case, might, if he wished, send it on to the province chief. The province chief would then review the case, and if he concurred with the warden he could forward the petition to the minister of defense in Saigon. The minister would have to approve the petition before the prisoner's status could be altered. The precise details of how all this *might* occur probably were unimportant as I was never able to learn of a single case where it actually *did* occur. Too many harried officials and too much bureaucratic paper-shuffling were involved to permit the policy to be workable. The policy was there, but the requirements for its implementation effectively precluded its producing any results.

Though government policy prevented exceptions being made in cases of prisoners of war, occasionally the Vietnamese found ways of handling them "informally." More than once I heard of a province or Chieu Hoi chief escorting a Vietcong, usually a crying child, into the Chieu Hoi Center and presiding over his instatement as a returnee. This "enemy" had been captured and was about to be sent to a prisoner of war camp before his timely "kidnapping" by the official. Even though he had not yet been officially designated a prisoner of war, his removal to the Chieu Hoi Center was most emphatically prohibited. The official involved ran no small risk, but he obviously thought that the case warranted such a risk. I agreed, and in one such instance I found myself entering a detention camp and coming away with a ragged, terrified, thirteen-year-old boy whom I put into my jeep and drove to the Chieu Hoi Center at great speed.

Once a Vietcong arrived at the Chieu Hoi Center, his/her status bore only a superficial resemblance to that of a prisoner. The center in Go Cong, like those in other provinces, was surrounded by defense barriers, but the intent was more to protect the returnees from outside threats rather than to guard them. Attacks presented a much more realistic threat to centers than did infiltrations. In 1969 there were thirty separate attacks upon centers; some deaths and numerous casualties resulted among the returnees. In fact, the returnees were quite free to wander around the center at will, and even to leave it for excursions into the immediate vicinity. It was necessary to secure a pass from the Chieu Hoi chief for trips

With the Dragon's Children

into town or anywhere in the province, but in my experience such passes were readily forthcoming.

Returnees were encouraged to visit their families. In cases where the family lived some distance away, frequently the wife and children would move into the center and take up residence with the returnee. There was little to prevent a returnee from simply walking away. He was not under guard and he wore no distinctive clothes or insignia. The only deterrent was his knowledge that he might be stopped by the local police and asked for his identification. He would not receive the necessary identification until after he had completed his stay at the center. In itself, the returnee's situation was almost always enough to prevent him from simply walking away; if he left before completing his stay, he would find himself abandoned and regarded as an enemy by both sides.

When the returnees in Go Cong sought a little amusement and the chance to spend some time away from the center, their most frequent destination was a small tea shop right next to the center. They could visit the tea shop without a pass, and it was a rare day when most of them didn't show up there at one time or another. The tea shop was a rickety old shed with walls of wood and a roof that consisted of equal amounts of tin and open air. When the sun shone, all eyes were blinded, and when it rained it was necessary to constantly rearrange the chairs and tables to avoid getting more than thoroughly damp.

The owner of the shop was called *Ong Chu* ("Mr. Uncle"). His customers tended to be a motley, hard-luck group, rather in keeping with the décor of the shop. Mr. Uncle kept a little book for the benefit of those customers who couldn't always pay their bill. He would enter the amount in his book, and the customer would sign his name and pay Mr. Uncle whenever he was able. The returnees were Mr. Uncle's best customers and also made up the largest contingent in the little worn book.[17] As Mr. Chu always had a smile on his face, he didn't appear to

- 45 -

David J. Garms

be overly concerned about getting his money from the returnees. After I began to know the returnees I would often go with them to Mr. Uncle's tea shop for a bowl of soup or some tea, coffee, or beer.

The most common refreshment was rice wine. Each town and hamlet had its own special method of fermenting whole rice to produce a local version of this deadly brew. Called *ba xi de, ru trang,* or *ru de,* rice wine was a genuine bargain in Go Cong. Though it cost the equivalent of a fraction of a cent a glass, it was also what must be the world's worst-tasting drink. It had a smell similar to that of kerosene and, given a choice, one might be wiser to choose kerosene over it.

Convention required that the wine be gulped; leisurely sipping was not condoned. The wine burned the throat and scorched a path all the way down to the stomach. This was just the beginning of the repercussions. The next day it was common to come down with stomach cramps, a headache, and diarrhea or even possibly all three of the latter problems at once. At this point the victim was likely to hope for a merciful death, but he would have to curse the fact that, whatever else rice wine might do, it was never known to be fatal.

When I went with a group of returnees to Mr. Uncle's tea shop, we would sit at a small circular table. Mr. Uncle would bang a bottle of rice wine and a single glass on the table. One of the returnees would grab the bottle and pour a few ounces into the glass. Usually he was the senior (determined by a combination of age and position) of the returnees present. Ritual required that he hold up the glass and examine it in the sunlight. (Like vodka, rice wine is clear and without color.) The returnee would then propose a toast of friendship with anyone seated at the table. He would take a gulp in the approved manner and hand the glass to the person he had chosen. Another person would then choose someone with whom to share a toast. The toasts of friendship would continue

- 46 -

With the Dragon's Children

until everyone had been included. Then it would become a free-for-all. Anyone could grab the bottle, pour wine into the glass, and propose a toast to anyone else. After everyone had been toasted a few times, the laughter would increase. Jokes and stories would be told and retold.

The returnees would often tell me how the Vietcong, with their typical thoroughness in finding a use for everything, encouraged their troops to drink rice wine just before a major engagement. This would make them more ferocious and courageous and, if they were wounded, they could continue to fight without suffering immediate pain.

Sometimes the returnees would drink with people of the town as well as with each other. I was rather surprised at first to observe the extent to which the people of Go Cong accepted the ex-Vietcong in their midst. Not only did they not appear to be troubled over the presence of the returnees, but they were inclined to mingle quite freely with them. In Go Cong, no special stigma was attached to the man or woman who had been a Vietcong. In fact, the whole problem of the Vietcong took on many of the aspects of being a "family affair." In some provinces, particularly the northernmost, members of the North Vietnamese Army (NVA) made up a small but very significant minority of the "enemy." This was not true in Go Cong, where the people could rightly regard the Vietcong as consisting, in the vast majority of cases, of their own "local boys." Very few people in Go Cong did not have a relative or a friend or a neighbor who was or who had been a Vietcong. Furthermore, a number of rather prominent citizens, primarily those connected with the various defense units and the Chieu Hoi Center itself, had once been Vietcong. Some of them had been truly dedicated to the Vietcong cause and had held important positions in the Vietcong organization. Such individuals tended to be men of more than ordinary intelligence and capabilities, and once they returned they often achieved positions of authority in the community. All this was known and accepted.

I became aware that returnees were not always so readily accepted in Saigon and in some of the other provinces. A few outside observers came to the conclusion that ex-Vietcong were more accepted in Go Cong, and also that Go Cong had been spared its fair share of the really heavy fighting, because the people of the province had achieved something of an "understanding" with the local Vietcong. Such observers pointed out that the forested area of southern Go Cong was being used by the Vietcong as a rest camp and staging ground for attacks on other provinces, and they suggested that the people of Go Cong knew this and might be tolerating it in return for being left out of major conflicts. This made for some fascinating conjecture, but as was the case with so many aspects of the war, the whole truth, if, indeed, there was one, defied certainty. It was true, however, that the people of Go Cong did not ordinarily attempt to draw a heavy, unwavering line between Vietcong and non-Vietcong. They left this, and the pursuit of whole truths, to the American, Hanoi, and South Vietnamese governments.

Even for the man who had not yet finished his stay at the center, and therefore was not yet entirely reinstated into the good graces of the GVN, acceptance by the people of the province was usually automatic. This tendency was encouraged by the fact that the returnees' appearance did not "mark" them in any way. Most returnees at the time of their arrival at the center were in great need of new clothing, and this was supplied them. The new clothes were essentially the same as those they had worn as Vietcong – a pair of loose cotton trousers and a long-sleeved shirt, usually black. This was also the way in which many of the people in town dressed. In the matter of appearance alone, therefore, a returnee could not

With the Dragon's Children

readily be distinguished from an ordinary citizen, nor, for that matter, from an active Vietcong.

Go Cong, like other provinces, had women Vietcong. The Vietnamese told me that, as a result of increasing losses in their ranks in recent years, the Vietcong had been compelled to recruit more women and teen-age boys. Whatever the cause, records of the Chieu Hoi Program did show that such persons were accounting for an increasingly large minority of the returnees. Even so, in Go Cong the number of women returnees was never great; there were only about twenty during the year I was there. Most of these women had been messengers and ammunition-bearers rather than combat troops. The situation was often different in the northernmost provinces of South Vietnam, where there had traditionally been more public support of the Vietcong and the North Vietnamese Army (NVA). In these provinces there were proportionally more women in Vietcong ranks and proportionally more in combat units. It was Chieu Hoi policy that women returnees be treated no differently from men. They received the same indoctrination and training and had the same responsibilities and restrictions. The only concession made to their sex was that they were furnished with separate living quarters.

Political re-indoctrination had always been an important part of the returnees' stay at the center. Except for occasional, vaguely worded directives from the Ministry of Chieu Hoi in Saigon, the various centers had been fairly free to develop their own courses. In 1968, the ministry rectified its lapse by issuing the circular "Standard Procedures for the Political Education of Hoi Chanh," and it immediately became the standard policy for political education courses at all Chieu Hoi Centers. (See Appendix I.)

Though the circular immediately became the official guide for courses in political indoctrination, several obstacles to complete compliance with it became obvious rather quickly.

- 49 -

David J. Garms

In the smaller centers, recommended supplies and qualified instructors were often not available. Where qualified instructors were present, many of them were never able to speak to the returnees in a manner which most of them could fully comprehend. Most returnees were simply never able to digest the majority of the material to which they were exposed. Finally, the circular was not published until after the Chieu Hoi Program had already been in operation for five years, with the result that it was in some cases difficult to adopt it in all details.

I had thought that it would be difficult if not impossible to change the attitudes of the returnees in the space of two months. It amazed me that the returnees seemed able to cope with such a drastic upheaval in their lives with little discernible psychological or emotional torment. It appeared to me that most of the returnees were able to accept what they were told in the political education course with no undue strain. For a time I wondered if the returnees really did believe all of it, or if they perhaps might be doing a remarkably clever job of faking acceptance.

As usual, I eventually came to believe that the truth stood in neither corner. The returnees were neither believing nor faking belief or a set of values so much as they were simply being realistic about their situation. They were accustomed to being told what to believe, and they were also accustomed to giving the appearance of believing what they were told, not so much out of deviousness as pragmatism. After all, the Vietcong had subjected them to a barrage of propaganda too. The GVN political education program, however much it differed in content, did not really differ all that much in form.

Again, the returnee was given "indisputable" evidence that one side was absolutely assured of victory in the end. Again, he was exhorted to express himself freely so that he might come to understand the "truth." Again, he was expected

With the Dragon's Children

to regard his instructors as affectionate big brothers who were devoting themselves to his best interests. Again, he was organized into special groups such as cells and teams. Again, he could be assured that any errors in his thinking would be carefully uncovered and laid before him so that his mind would be freer to accept the "truth." Again, there was an intricate system of rewards and punishments to help him along the path to enlightenment. The returnee had been through all this before, and to him it was the retelling of an old, old story.

In the majority of cases, the returnees did not so much change their beliefs as they simply had no strong beliefs to be changed. The returnees had specific grievances and aspirations, but on a broader level they were simply apolitical. The real interests and loyalties of the rural Vietnamese as a whole rested with themselves and their families and with their villages. At most, they might feel personal loyalty to their district or province. A more encompassing sense of identity rarely existed. To try and foster in them a broader loyalty, such as toward a nation, was to attempt to implant a concept in the mind for which there was no corresponding emotion in the heart. They could not personally identify with either Saigon or Hanoi, and being able to see themselves as part of a worldwide power struggle between communism and capitalism was beyond them. They wanted, above all, to be left alone.

The essential apolitical nature of many Vietnamese can help explain some of the unusual phenomena of the war. For example, it no longer seemed quite so remarkable that a man could change sides with apparent ease when it's accepted that he hadn't really believed what he had been told before and wasn't going to really believe what he was hearing now. He might have been the most courageous of warriors for one side, and now, a matter of perhaps weeks or months later, he was prepared to fight just as tenaciously for the other side. It is unrealistic to suppose that this change must necessarily have

David J. Garms

been solely political in nature. An appreciation for the essential apolitical nature of rural Vietnamese can also shed some light on the common argument over whether the Vietnamese are able warriors or not. Often it appeared to depend most on where they were fighting. A member of a local militia would sometimes display ferocious courage in the defense of his own village or town. However, if he was put in an ARVN uniform and sent to fight in another province or in a neighboring country, the same fighting spirit might not be as evident. He could not identify with a nation as he could with a village, and being ordered to fight in the name of an entire country often failed to inspire him to the same degree. It is also due to their limited sense of identity that most Vietnamese viewed the presence of American troops in Vietnam with both mistrust and amusement. "Why," many people in Go Cong asked, "should you fight when neither your town nor your province nor even your country is under attack?" Any attempt to mumble something about doing it for the good of the Vietnamese people was greeted with laughter and complete disbelief. They themselves, as they pointed out to me, would never presume to cross the ocean to defend *my* village. At least in Go Cong, gratitude was not the most typical characteristic of the reaction of the people to the U.S. presence. (It is interesting to note that after the fall of South Vietnam in 1975, the new government launched a "political" training program for all who worked for the GVN.)

In addition to political education (and perhaps considerably more to their personal benefit), the returnees received some vocational training while they were at the center. Before Trieu's arrival, this phase of the program had been badly neglected. Recognizing the potential value of a strong vocational training program both to the returnees and to the province, Trieu made efforts to expand the training available to the returnees, and I encouraged his efforts.

With the Dragon's Children

A young man named Nguyen Van Ha was appointed chief of the vocational training section.[18] Ha had been a tailor for the Vietcong.[19] He was a conscientious young man, very proud of his skill as a tailor, and very willing to teach some of this skill to the returnees. Many times Ha offered to do some tailoring for me. He would never accept any money in return, nor did he ever imply that favors would be expected as payment. Ha's assistant in the vocational training section was Le Van Khai. A very quiet man in his mid-forties, Khai had been a carpenter in the Vietcong. In addition to teaching carpentry to the returnees, he was constantly going about on his own, repairing furniture, doors, and windows at the center. He never complained about anything and never asked for time off. Khai was something of a chronic worker.

Until Trieu assigned Ha and Khai to the vocational training section, the only man in the section had been a barber. The barber too had been a Vietcong. In addition to teaching his trade to the returnees, he was allowed to practice it in the center for profit as it was convenient to have a barber in residence and his prices were lower than those in town. The first time I sought his services, I was more than a trifle nervous. On a Sunday morning shortly after my arrival in Go Cong, I walked over to the center to see what was happening. Nothing was happening except for the barber giving haircuts to the returnees. There was no one around from the staff. I decided to get in line with the returnees. When my turn came I sat back in the chair. After he finished cutting my hair, the barber asked me if I would like a shave too. I had become very relaxed sitting back in the chair, not thinking about anything in particular. I said, "Sure, I'd like a shave too." The barber began to shave my face, and suddenly I realized where I was. There was no one at the center except for the barber and the returnees and me. I was sitting in a chair, surrounded by men who had all been Vietcong. The barber put his hands on my

- 53 -

forehead and pushed back my head to shave my throat. I held my breath, but I was determined not to panic in front of the returnees. The barber was very, very careful not to make even the slightest nick. When I got up I saw that he was sweating as much as I.

We were somewhat hampered in our efforts to improve the center because, although the Chieu Hoi Program was a GVN program, it did not always enjoy GVN's unequivocal support. Though implemented by GVN, the program was largely initiated and financed by the United States, and some Vietnamese officials regarded it as being almost exclusively for U.S. interests. Those officials who could not be persuaded of the worth of the program for humanitarian reasons, however, could sometimes be induced to support it for more practical ones. They could appreciate that the program was reducing the manpower of the Vietcong and adding to the manpower resources of GVN. They were impressed by the value of the returnees or intelligence purposes. They became increasingly interested when they realized that the returnees were bringing in with them valuable weapons and materials. By developing a system of cash awards, the government began to officially encourage the returnees to bring in such things.

Though previous lists had been in use, GVN published its most comprehensive list of cash awards for the return of weapons and various other materials in 1970.[20] The following is an incomplete but representative reproduction of the document. The amounts that are shown are in U.S. dollar equivalents according to the official rate of exchange in effect at that time (though, only a few months after the document was published, the official rate of exchange was changed, and each cash award was then worth about half the previous amount in terms of U.S. dollars).

With the Dragon's Children

WEAPON	CASH AWARD
pistol: all types	$10.00
rifle: all types	$25.00
submachine gun: all types	$42.00
light machine gun: all types	$84.00
heavy machine gun: .30 caliber	$146.00
heavy machine gun: .50 caliber	$168.00
anti-tank gun: 14.5 mm.	$336.00
anti-aircraft gun: all types	$336.00
rocket launcher: B 40 or 41	$84.00
rocket launcher: 122 mm.	$84.00
mortar tube: 81 or 82 mm.	$252.00

AMMUNITION AND EXPLOSIVES	
hand grenade: one	$1.60
antitank mine: one	$34.00
plastic: one kilo	$8.40
TNT: one kilo	$4.00
mortar round: one 81 or 82 mm.	$12.40

COMMUNICATIONS EQUIPMENT	
field operations radio: Chinese made	$67.00
telephone station: central unit	$126.00
generator: under 5 kw.	$84.00
generator: over 5 kw.	$168.00

FOOD

David J. Garms

rice: 100 kilos	$8.40
salt: 100 kilos	$8.40

If a returnee was able to bring in only a major part of a weapon, he would receive a cash award varying from fifty percent to eighty percent of the award allowed for the entire weapon. For example, a returnee would receive $20 for a rifle breech as opposed to $25 for the entire rifle. A returnee bringing in the breech of a .50 caliber machine gun would receive $84 instead of $168 for the whole machine gun. If a returnee did not personally bring the weapons or other equipment in, by leading GVN or Allied Forces to their location he would be eligible for a cash award equal to one-third of the amount he would have received for bringing them in himself. If he was not personally able to lead the operation because of wounds or illness, by informing GVN or Allied Forces of their location he would still receive a reward equal to one-fifth of the original amount.

One of the weapons typically used by the Vietcong was the AK-47, an assault rifle. Originally it was a Russian-made weapon (designed by a Russian weapons engineer named Mikhail Kalashikov) but later factories for its production were established in China and other countries, with only a few of the original Russian-made ones still in use. The weapon was well-adapted for guerrilla warfare. It could be dropped in dirt and/or water and would still fire, unlike the American-made M-16, which would jam if subjected to harsh conditions. The bayonet attached to the AK-47 barrel could be released from its retracted position with a flick of the wrist. The Vietcong soldier typically arranged a harness across his back and chest with up to six magazines holding thirty cartridges each. Although the M-16 was the deadlier of the two weapons, many

With the Dragon's Children

American troops admired the sturdiness and reliability of the AK-47.

The returnees frequently brought in AK-47s with them. One returnee who did so was Manh. He was immensely proud of his fine weapon and of his ability to use it. Of course, he was required to turn it over to the staff when he first came to the center. Trieu sometimes carried the weapon with him when he made trips into the field. One day I was going to go to one of the districts to buy sand for construction at the center. I looked around, saw Manh standing nearby, and asked for him to accompany me. (I rarely traveled outside the town without a Vietnamese with me; even in Go Cong, a lone, unarmed American would be taking unwarranted risks.) Manh and I climbed into the truck, and then Trieu, who knew I didn't carry a weapon, handed me the AK-47 to take along. For a moment I sat there in the driver's seat holding the weapon. I glanced at Manh sitting next to me and then, with as much nonchalance as I could muster, I handed him the weapon. For the rest of the day Manh rode "shotgun" with the same weapon he had carried in the Vietcong ranks. He was proud and contented as the two of us bounced down the dusty roads. If I had not permitted him to carry the weapon he would have recognized that I mistrusted him. Instead, it was up to him to prove that he was as trustworthy as I assumed him to be. I probably could not have had a more dedicated bodyguard than Manh that day.

CHAPTER IV

Of Hearts and Minds

During the war the world concerned itself with "winning the hearts and minds" of the Vietnamese people. Therefore, it is reasonable to consider in particular what was in the hearts and minds of those among them who had managed to be "won" by both sides. As I talked more with the returnees in Go Cong, I began to isolate some fairly specific reasons which had motivated them to become Vietcong. With no attempt to list them in order of importance, the reasons are briefly as follows:

(1) <u>Conscription</u>. About half the returnees in Go Cong told me that they had been forced to become Vietcong. Though this was undoubtedly true in a number of cases, it was to the advantage of the returnees to declare they had joined the Vietcong only under force, and therefore this explanation had to be viewed with caution.

(2) <u>To correct injustices</u>. A few returnees held broad humanistic views, but in most cases it was more a matter of personal grievances. To the impoverished peasant who had never owned the land he worked, the Vietcong promise of extensive land reform was definitely appealing. The man

With the Dragon's Children

who felt government leaders had not treated him fairly was also impressed with the Vietcong promise of equality for all. This category would include the man whose home had been destroyed or his family killed by GVN or U.S. forces.

(3) The opportunity to lead an adventuresome life. This appeal was particularly marked in the cases of very young returnees. One such returnee expressed this very well: "I loved being a soldier. I liked the weapon they gave me and really got a kick out of firing it into villages. I liked watching our mortars land on a town, hearing them explode and the noise of buildings crumbling, then wondering how much damage we had done."

(4) Belief in an ultimate Vietcong victory. No one likes to be on the losing side, and certainly the Vietnamese were not immune to this type of reasoning. Particularly in areas where the Vietcong presence was major, there was enormous pressure on the individual to "get on the bandwagon." Bombarded with propaganda and often living in a small, isolated village, it was frequently difficult for a peasant to get a clear picture of what was happening nationwide. He was therefore inclined to believe that the side which was winning his village must also be winning the country.

(5) To overthrow the government. This reason, a historical one, would only be applicable to Vietnamese of a certain age. The majority of Vietnamese had never supported French rule and, with the close of World War II, had anticipated obtaining their freedom as a nation. They had reason to expect that the United States would support them in this. During the war the United States, as a countermeasure to Japanese expansion, had encouraged the growing nationalistic movement in Indochina. In fact, some of the U.S. forces had even assisted in the training of Vietnamese guerrillas under the leadership of Ho Chi Minh and Vo Nguyen Giap.[21] Shortly after the defeat of Japan, Ho Chi Minh began writing letters to

- 59 -

President Truman asking for the support of the United States against the restoration of French colonial rule. The events that followed must have surprised and embittered the old man in Hanoi, turning him resolutely anti-American; his letters were unanswered, the French returned, fighting broke out, and the United States eventually came in on the side of the French. The native resistance movement, Vietnam Doc Lap Dong Minh (usually shortened to Vietminh), had wide support among the Vietnamese people, many of whom regarded it more as representing liberation than communism. After independence and partition in 1954, some of the original followers of the Vietminh joined its successor, the Vietcong movement. We occasionally received into the center individuals whose careers as guerrillas spanned more than twenty years and who had begun them with the Vietminh.

(6) <u>To protest the policies of the Diem government</u>. This reason was also essentially historical. The French had won the support of the United States in their attempt to re-establish colonial rule over Vietnam partially by claiming that the Vietminh movement was a case of Communist aggression. (The reasoning being that if South Vietnam fell then other countries in Indochina would also fall. This became known as the "domino effect".) Taking his cue from this, Diem later made the same claim in regard to the Vietcong and so, once again, U.S. assistance was forthcoming. To a significant number of Vietnamese, rule by Diem was hardly more acceptable than rule by the French, particularly after 1956, when he refused to allow the national election provided for by the Geneva Accords. The growing presence of the United States served to polarize the situation. Caught between the United States-supported Diem government and the burgeoning Vietcong movement, the Vietnamese were denied the option of a third choice or the luxury of remaining neutral. When it became a choice of supporting Diem or joining the Vietcong, Vietnamese

With the Dragon's Children

began choosing the latter in increasing numbers during the early years of U.S. involvement. As a result, at the Chieu Hoi Center in Go Cong, we received a number of returnees who had joined the Vietcong during the Diem regime.

(7) Belief in the Communist ideology. Some of the returnees stated that they had become Vietcong because they believed in communism. However, when pressed to give an explanation of Communist ideology, very few of them were able to do more than mumble a few words about promises of "justice" for everyone," "land owned by the people," "no more wars," and "freedom." Virtually none of them had any idea to what extent these promises had, in fact, been kept by North Vietnam. There were a few who could grasp the essentials of communism and who sincerely believed in it, but in Go Cong they were very, very few. As the GVN made the same promises, the allegiance of the average person depended to a considerable extent on who reached him first.

These were the most common explanations that the returnees gave me for having become Vietcong. The divisions are somewhat arbitrary, as most of the returnees seemed to have been influenced by a combination of factors.

The returnees in Go Cong were also very willing to tell me their reasons for having left the Vietcong. The following are the reasons I was given most often:

(1) Fear. This was the response I was given more frequently than any other. The Vietcong recruit or conscript did indeed have a great deal to fear: there was the fear of being killed, wounded, or captured by the GVN or Allied Forces; the fear of bringing retaliation down upon your family and property; and the fear of dying far from home without a proper burial. Naturally, it was the young Vietcong who was most often the victim of these fears. It was rare that fear alone could bring in an ideologically-motivated Vietcong.

- 61 -

David J. Garms

The same young man who had said he joined the Vietcong because "I loved being a soldier," offered the following explanation for returning to the GVN. "One day I saw some of my Vietcong friends killed. Those helicopter gunships are terrible. I decided I didn't want to fight any more. I didn't want to die." Danger, of course, was relative, for a man could be killed, wounded, or captured fighting with the GVN as well as with the Vietcong. Fear became the dominant factor when an individual believed that one side offered him greater *relative* safety than the other.

(2) <u>Hardship</u>. Life was not easy in the Vietcong ranks. The returnees mentioned poor or inadequate shelter, food, clothing, and medical care. Some referred to the discipline as having been harsh and said that they had been under constant surveillance. Many mentioned their dislike for having to be always hiding, always on the move. Those who had been with the Vietcong for a long time said that these hardships had increased in recent years. Along with fear, however, hardship was rarely a major factor in the decision of a dedicated, veteran Vietcong to return to the GVN.

(3) <u>Homesickness</u>. Vietnamese, particularly those from rural areas, were very much dependent upon their families and villages for their sense of identity. The returnees who had served most of their time with the Vietcong far from their homes said that they had suffered terrible anxiety over the welfare of their families and villages. Those returnees who had been Vietcong for a considerable period of time remarked that in recent years they were forced to be on the move increasingly and had been able to visit their homes less frequently. Again, the really hardcore Vietcong were not likely to be influenced by this factor alone to any great degree.

(4) <u>Loss of belief in an ultimate Vietcong victory.</u> A man who had chosen a side partially because he thought it would be the winning one is understandably prone (particularly in the

With the Dragon's Children

absence of a third course—neutrality) to change sides when he can no longer believe it. Even returnees who had been Vietcong for a long time were inclined to return to the GVN partially for this reason. However, as the evidence of "who's winning" showed an inclination to vary from district to district and even from week to week, there is no reason to assume that, when people base their loyalty on such evidence, their loyalty could not possibly shift when the evidence does.

(5) Loss of faith in the Vietcong cause. Some returnees had left the Vietcong when they grew tired of waiting for the promises to be kept. They did not see that they were any closer to peace, prosperity, or equality by supporting the Vietcong cause. Some of them came to disagree that, in the interests of a better Vietnam, it was necessary to kill so many Vietnamese. A few were partially aware of North Vietnam's course of development and could not believe that this represented a substantial improvement over their life in South Vietnam. This loss-of-faith factor was the most important in the case of a veteran, politically-committed Vietcong who decided to desert the cause. As such a person tended to be better-educated and more politically-oriented to begin with, he must have usually come to such a decision by means of his own reasoning rather than as a result of the GVN propaganda.

These were the reasons the returnees gave me most frequently for their having left the Vietcong.[22] These reasons are consistent with the finding in a nationwide evaluation of the Chieu Hoi program funded by the Department of Defence.[23] In the majority of cases it was a matter of a combination of these factors influencing them. Once a Vietcong, whatever his reasons, had decided to leave the Vietcong, and subsequently had completed his stay at the center, there were a number of courses open to him as far as his future was concerned. There were both advantages and drawbacks to each of the courses.

David J. Garms

The following is a brief list of the important courses of action open to a returnee after he left the center:

(1)   Return home and resume whatever occupation had been followed

before. In the vast majority of cases, this meant returning to a hamlet and becoming a farmer again. In a fair number of cases this was not a valid option as it presupposed that the war had left the returnee with a home and a family to which he could return. Even when a returnee could go home, he often would not. His fear of retaliation from his former comrades was not necessarily an exaggerated one. In a small village where the GVN presence was minor or nonexistent and where everyone's past was common knowledge, it could be dangerous indeed to be a returnee. Even the family of a returnee might not be safe. A returnee named Chat told me of being part of a group of Vietcong who came to a village in Hoa Dong District one night to assassinate the wife of a returnee: "It was horrible. The commander just shot her down with a hand pistol. He was going to kill the children too, but I persuaded him not to. I hid the children, and then went to find their father. I had decided that I could no longer be a Vietcong." Nevertheless, rural Vietnamese identified with a particular locality so closely that some returnees elected to return to their villages.

(2)   Resettle in another area. The returnee could feel somewhat safer if he elected to act on this option, though there was always the possibility that the Vietcong in the area in which he settled would learn of his past. Returnees who wanted to achieve the greatest possible anonymity would join the ranks of the refugees swelling the populations of the major cities. The option of moving to another place had the significant disadvantage of uprooting the returnee from his original surroundings and friends with which he was familiar and upon which he was accustomed to depending. Because of the Vietnamese tendency to identify strongly with a particular

With the Dragon's Children

locality, many of the returnees were reluctant to move far away.

(3) <u>Settle in a Chieu Hoi hamlet</u>. Recognizing the problems of the returnees in resettling, the GVN established a program for the development of new hamlets in many provinces. These hamlets were to be populated entirely by returnees. Until such a hamlet had become self-sufficient, it was to be provided with material and financial support. The program allowed for the establishment of forty hamlets, each with provision for a hundred returnees and their families. This particular option was not available to returnees in Go Cong until the establishment of the first hamlet there in 1969. However, some returnees informed me that they would not move into a Chieu Hoi hamlet even if one already existed as they thought such a hamlet would present a severe temptation for Vietcong attack.

(4) <u>Join some form of military or quasi-military organization</u>. Even though their status as returnees entitled them to an automatic one-year deferment, this is what the majority of returnees in Go Cong elected to do.[24] There were a number of such organizations open to them: the national army (ARVN); local military and quasi-military units such as the Popular Forces, the Regional Forces, the Rural Development Team, and the APT; and a special program known as the Kit Carson Scouts, which consisted of returnees who were attached to a number of U.S. combat units as scouts.

Returnees elected to join such organizations because, except for ARVN, it enabled them to stay close to home, because it offered the most readily available means of gaining minimally-decent employment, and because, as it meant that they would be armed and surrounded by armed men, it represented relatively greater security from Vietcong retaliation. Some organizations, such as the APT and the Kit Carson Scouts, were composed entirely of returnees.[25] (The name

- 65 -

originated from American Indian scouts who led the U.S. Army units on the frontier.) Even if a returnee joined one of the other organizations open to him, he might well find himself serving along with some of the same comrades he had known in the Vietcong ranks. Upon leaving the center in Go Cong, roughly seventy percent of the returnees once more bore arms, though this time for the GVN.

Examples of why Vietnamese became Vietcong, why they left the Vietcong, and the kinds of futures that awaited them can best be illustrated by a few but very representative case histories. I compiled the following five representative case histories from returnees whom I came to know well as Chieu Hoi advisor in Go Cong.

NGUYEN VAN MANH

Background: Manh was twenty-five and single when he came to the center in 1967. He was the son of a tenant farmer in Dong Xon Village, Hoa Dong District. As a child he had herded the village buffaloes and cared for his father's duck flock. Manh first became a Vietcong in 1964, and returned to the GVN the following year. He returned to Dong Xon and became a Vietcong again almost immediately.[26] In late 1967 he left the Vietcong once more and again went through the Go Cong Chieu Hoi Center's political education course.

Personality: Manh was unconcerned about any of life's larger questions. He was poorly motivated and content to merely react to situations. He preferred activities with a few close friends and did not intermingle freely with the other returnees. He tried to avoid work and said that his Vietcong comrades had severely criticized him for this. He habitually went about the center with his mouth open and a blank stare

With the Dragon's Children

on his face. Actually, Manh was a good deal more intelligent than his manner would indicate.

Reasons for Joining the Vietcong: "The first time, I didn't know why. The second time, I was forced to join again or be killed."

Reasons for Leaving the Vietcong: "The life was too hard and too dangerous. I didn't care about the things they told me. I didn't want to die."

Aftermath: After completing the course at the center for the second time, Manh joined the APT rather than return to his village.

LE VAN TU

Background: Tu was forty-eight, married, and had three children. He had owned a tea shop and his wife was an excellent seamstress. Together they had made a comfortable living in Tan Thanh Village, Hoa Lac District. During the Diem regime of the early 1960s, Tu became a Vietcong intelligence liaison officer. He continued to work with intelligence for the Vietcong until his return to the GVN early in 1968.

Personality: Tu was a gentleman and very intelligent. He appeared to be almost too academically oriented for a rural Vietnamese. He was always the first to read any new books and magazines at the center. He was not easily convinced of anything; power could not sway him as much as logic. Tu strongly disciplined himself in both mind and body. He ate lightly and seldom consumed alcohol. He was devoted to his family and friends, but it was difficult for a stranger to win his confidence. His stare was very intense, and he always appeared to study a person before beginning a conversation with him. Most of the other returnees were distinctly uneasy in his presence.

David J. Garms

Reasons for Joining the Vietcong: "The Vietcong were strong in my village. I was urged to cooperate, but I also thought that I should. I could not support President Diem, and I had to support someone. I was selected to be the intelligence liaison officer in the areas of the district that were controlled by the GVN as I was respected and it was thought that no one would be suspicious of me."

Reasons for Leaving the Vietcong: "I became increasingly nervous about my situation as the GVN became stronger in the area. I was afraid that someone would eventually tell the GVN authorities about me and that I would be killed. I didn't want to die and leave my family alone. I also began to wonder if the Vietcong were right. I began to question everything. Finally, I could go on no longer, and there was no other course but to return to the GVN."

Aftermath: After leaving the center Tu did not wish to return to his village, which was still not under effective GVN control at night. He and his family settled in the first Chieu Hoi hamlet in Go Cong as soon as it opened in 1969. His wife continued to work as a seamstress, and Tu became foreman of one of the center's work teams. Friends in Go Cong informed me that, in 1970, Tu was struck and instantly killed by a truck that was passing by the center.

NGUYEN VAN TAM

Background: Tam was thirty-five, married, and had two children. He was the son of a laborer and part-time fisherman from Binh Xuan Village, Hoa Tan District. As a teenager Tam had joined the Vietminh in the early 1950s. Later he became the platoon leader of a Vietcong unit operating in northern Go Cong and parts of eastern Dinh Tuong Province. Tam ended seventeen years as a guerrilla when he became a returnee late in 1967.

With the Dragon's Children

Personality: Tam had always had to struggle. Even as a child he was required to do heavy labor to help support his family. His face and hands revealed years of hard work, but the strain rarely showed in his manner. His friendliness and sense of humor made him popular with everyone. He was also very athletic, and everyone always wanted him to be on their volleyball team. Tam was highly respected by both the returnees and the staff. He was a natural leader of the poor and the deprived.

Reasons for Joining the Vietcong: "I thought it would lead to a better life for everyone. I fought first with the Vietminh and then with the Vietcong because I thought that only they could help the people."

Reasons for Leaving the Vietcong: "The Vietminh defeated the French, but the Vietcong failed to win anything. They did not keep their promises. I was tired of killing people whom I had really wanted to help. After so many years of sacrifice, my own condition was more and more miserable. Nothing at all had improved for anyone."

Aftermath: Tam became a platoon leader and a very valued member of the APT.

LE VAN DAU

Background: Dau was fifty years old, married, and the father of four children. He was the son of a tenant farmer in Vinh Huu Village, Hoa Binh District. His parents had been dead for many years. As his own health was not good, Dau was not able to perform heavy labor. He was a fairly skilled cabinetmaker, and by this means was able to obtain a meager income. He allowed his three daughters to move about freely, but he hid his sixteen-year-old son at night so that the Vietcong would not find him when they came to recruit men from his village. Otherwise, Dau cooperated with the Vietcong. He gave them any food he had and helped disseminate Vietcong printed propaganda.

Personality: Dau was a sensitive, kindly old gentleman. He was a devout Buddhist and earnestly applied religious principles to everyday life. He was unflinchingly honest, but he was easily intimidated by a display of power, and it was easy for people to take advantage of him. Despite his poor health, he worked very hard at everything he did. When he came to the center he began sweeping the floors and sidewalks early each morning without being asked to do it. He deeply loved his family and friends. When he was saddened for any reason his eyes filled with tears very easily. He tried to be helpful to everyone and to avoid trouble as much as he could.

Reasons for Joining the Vietcong: "The Vietcong were strong in my village. I was afraid that if I did not cooperate with them they might harm my wife and children. I had no choice."

Reasons for Leaving the Vietcong: "I was afraid of being killed by the GVN soldiers for having associated with the Vietcong. I was afraid the Vietcong would find my son and take him with them."

Aftermath: I got Dau a job gardening and doing maintenance in the CORDS compound. He worked hard at his job and appeared very happy with it. The Americans grew very fond of the old man, and they would often give him food and pieces of clothing. Dau asked for nothing, though, and perhaps this is what so impressed the Americans. One day in the CORDS compound an American said to me, "Everyone in this country has his hand out, but there's that old guy over there who wants nothing but to be left alone to live his life."

With the Dragon's Children

LE NGOC DUC

<u>Background:</u> Duc was fourteen years old. His father died when he was an infant, and his mother provided for him by working for tenant farmers in their fields. The hamlet in which Duc and his mother lived in Hoa Binh District was under partial Vietcong control. Duc became a Vietcong early in 1967. Late in the same year he turned himself over to the district Chieu Hoi chief of Hoa Binh.

<u>Personality:</u> Duc was very much a child and was easily led by anyone. He had no comprehension at all of the conflict in Vietnam. However, he was quite eager to learn, and he asked many pertinent questions during his stay at the center. He was not reluctant to mingle freely with the other returnees, even the older, tougher ones. Duc enrolled in vocational training classes. He became reasonably proficient at tailoring and even took up typing. He was unnaturally serious for his age, but he was well-liked and treated very kindly by everyone.

<u>*Reasons for Joining the Vietcong:*</u> "They made me."

<u>*Reasons for Leaving the Vietcong:*</u> "I was afraid I would be killed."

<u>Aftermath:</u> During his stay at the center, many people in town took an interest in him. After he left the center, one such person—a man named Duc-Ba, who had himself been a Vietcong[27]— took Duc to live with him. Given enough time to finish growing up, Duc showed promise of becoming quite a fine man.

CHAPTER V

"Will You Eat Dog Meat?"

From the beginning, I had been able to get along with most of the staff quite well. It took somewhat longer to establish a good relationship with the returnees. I almost despaired, though, of ever being able to accomplish anything with the APT members.

Trieu had succeeded in bringing the APT under control, but they were still the toughest lot of men I ever encountered. They were all, of course, ex-Vietcong. One of the options open to returnees who had completed their stay at the center was to apply for the APT. Characteristically, the returnees who had been among the fiercest of the Vietcong and who had served in combat units were the ones who applied for it. It was a very rugged outfit and had a great deal of *esprit de corps*. Their responsibility as a major disseminator of GVN propaganda necessitated their spending a large proportion of their time in highly contested areas. They were well-armed for the purpose of being able to defend themselves. In the case of the APT, however, a clear distinction between defense and offense was not always made. Until Trieu came to the center, the APT in

With the Dragon's Children

Go Cong had displayed a marked proclivity for hunting down and killing their former comrades.

One of the most important responsibilities of the APT was to distribute propaganda leaflets throughout the province. The most common leaflet displayed the flags of the GVN and all its allies, and directed in Vietnamese, English, Thai, and Korean that this leaflet was to be honored as a safe conduct pass for its bearer. Vietcong wishing to become returnees were to be received as such immediately upon their showing this leaflet. Other leaflets explained the purpose of the Chieu Hoi Program and exhorted the Vietcong to turn themselves in and become part of it. The returnees became part of the leaflet propaganda effort too; they wrote out personal statements urging their former comrades to return as they had done. Still other leaflets stressed the factors that were known to motivate Vietcong to return: fear, hardships, homesickness, and disillusionment. Leaflets having nationwide appeal were produced by the Ministry of Chieu Hoi and the Ministry of Information in coordination with JUSPAO. Leaflets produced at the local level (for which funds were provided in the Chieu Hoi budget) usually dealt with specific returnees—their reasons for returning to the GVN, their impressions of the Chieu Hoi Program, and personal appeals to their former comrades to return.

Not content with hand distribution, the United States launched a major program of dropping enormous quantities of all types of leaflets from airplanes and helicopters. In one month alone, (May 1969) a total of 713.4 million leaflets were dropped. One could imagine the confusion of villagers in contested areas whenever they heard an airplane or helicopter approaching; would this particular plane rain down upon them bombs or pieces of paper?

The Vietcong too made extensive use of leaflet propaganda. Some of their leaflets described the great number of GVN and U.S. troops killed or wounded and of the number

- 73 -

of weapons captured from them. Other leaflets proclaimed the "wrongs" of the GVN and of the American presence, and extolled the virtues of the Vietcong cause. Still others carried quotations from Ho Chi Minh. Many of the leaflets pinpointed specific villages, combat units, or government programs that had deserved the Vietcong's particular attention. Chieu Hoi Centers were frequently mentioned in this context. This leaflet warfare took on such proportions that it appeared to me that surely every single inhabitant of South Vietnam must have long since acquired his own complete collection of all leaflets produced by both sides.

The following are representative examples of leaflets produced by the GVN and the Vietcong which pertain to the Chieu Hoi Program:

GVN LEAFLET PRODUCED AT THE NATIONAL LEVEL
(7-738 SP 1832)

One side contains a sketch of a Vietcong soldier standing at a fork in the road. Written on one road is: "This is the road of death and destruction. If you want to die, then take this road." Written on the other road is: "This road will lead you to love, freedom, and happiness. You will be able to elect your own leaders. This is the road of life." On the bottom of the picture is the question: "Which road will you choose?"

On the other side of the leaflet is written: "A message to all friends on the other side. Whatever goals you are working for in the Vietcong, you will not be able to realize them. Your life is controlled and you must follow the dictates of your leaders. However, with the GVN there are elections so that you can choose your leaders to represent you."

With the Dragon's Children

GVN LEAFLET PRODUCED AT THE LOCAL LEVEL
(SP-2004)

On one side is a picture of returnee Nguyen Van Be sitting with his parents and five brothers after he completed his training at the Go Cong Chieu Hoi Center. Beside the picture is written: "Here Nguyen Van Be is relaxing with his family. Everyone can certainly see that he is alive and healthy. The Vietcong have lost face because they will never be willing to admit that after his return he is alive and well. What should we all think of this?"

The other side of the leaflet contains a hand-written statement:

"Dear all honorable people of this nation.

I am Nguyen Van Be. I am the son of Nguyen Van Hieu and Le Thi Ba. I was born in Kim Son Village of Dinh Tuong Province. I was captured by the Vietcong on May 30, 1966, and put into an infantry unit which operated throughout the Delta. I was an ordinary soldier and faced many hardships. I witnessed the deaths of many people and the destruction of many villages. I kept hoping for the day when I could escape. That day came, and now I am alive and happy under the GVN. I would like to encourage my friends in the Vietcong ranks to return to the GVN so that they might also have the opportunity to return before they are killed. With the GVN is the best way to build a nation."

(Signed) Nguyen Van Be
September 15, 1967

VIETCONG LEAFLET PICKED UP IN HOA BINH DISTRICT, GO CONG PROVINCE

"All Chieu Hoi returnees have betrayed and harmed the people. They are traitors to the cause and will be exterminated by the people sooner or later. In honor of Chairman Ho, all people must be determined to track down the traitors in our midst. We must go on to intensify our attacks on all fronts in order to destroy the grip of the Americans. Be confident that the National Liberation Front will be victorious in the upcoming rainy season."

VIETCONG LEAFLET PICKED UP IN HOA DONG
DISTRICT, GO CONG PROVINCE

"Hoa Dong's people are determined to develop their traditional resistance in order to exterminate Chieu Hoi traitors and to liberate hamlets under enemy domination. The puppet hamlet chiefs are the wicked henchmen of the Americans, and the people must punish them. Chairman Ho's request to perform missions for the Front will be honored by the people.

If only the henchmen of the Americans would come to know their mistakes and quit their work, which has betrayed and harmed the people and fatherland, the people would give them clemency."

In any case, neither the Vietcong nor the GVN could claim that they were the first to make use of written propaganda in Vietnam. There was a precedent. In the thirteenth century, the Vietnamese were independent, but they suffered heavy oppression. There was widespread misery and discontent. China chose this opportunity to try and regain control

With the Dragon's Children

of Vietnam, and a massive army was sent to achieve this end. One of the weapons the army carried with it was psychological warfare. The Chinese invaders attached posters to trees, passed out leaflets, and carved inscriptions on logs to be floated down streams, all of which stated that their only purpose in invading the country was to restore justice. Many Vietnamese were taken in by the propaganda campaign, and Vietnam was soon once again under Chinese domination.[28]

As the members of the APT in Go Cong worked directly with the Chieu Hoi Center, I thought it important that I get along with them. From the beginning, though, the team members gave me a rough time. This was particularly true of their leader, Tran Cong Bao, company commander of the APT in Go Cong Province. (*Bao* is pronounced the same as the English word *bough*.) He was a tall, husky man with a large head and massive jaw. Leadership was nothing new to Bao; he had been the commander of the Vietcong 206th Company, which operated in Go Cong and parts of adjoining Ding Tuong Province. I soon learned the story behind his leaving the Vietcong. He had gotten into an argument with the political commissar of the company.[29] The commissar, having more authority than even the company commander, overruled Bao. This was more than Bao could bear, and he immediately switched sides. He was a proud man and a dedicated fighter. People remarked to me that Bao never settled for anything less than the complete annihilation of whomever he was fighting. Also, he would accept authority from no one.[30] After returning to the GVN and finishing his re-indoctrination course, Bao was selected by the province chief to be the commander of the seventy-member APT company in Go Cong.[31]

After weeks of effort, I had almost given up trying to establish rapport with the members of the APT. Then, one day I happened to wander into Mr. Uncle's tea shop. I saw five APT members in quite a drunken state around one of the tables.

- 77 -

David J. Garms

One of them screamed at me, "You American bastard! Sit your ass down here and have a drink!"

I hesitated. These were fierce men under the best of circumstances, and now they were drunk. Finally, anger triumphed over fear and I sat down saying, "All right you bastards, let's drink!"

A moment later one of them asked me, "How many men have you killed?"

"None" I answered.

One APT member exclaimed, "That's stupid! This is a war, and you have to kill people!" (This caused me to ponder again the fact that these men seemed to retain no sentiment toward their former comrades.)

Indeed, the APT cheerfully hunted down their former comrades in arms whenever they could. Another team member said, "This policy of the Chieu Hoi ministry doesn't work. Look, I'm an ex-Vietcong and I know. We must hit the Vietcong hard. The blood must run before they understand that they must leave the Vietcong or die. Fear and power are the only things that count."

Another man muttered, "The way I like to let the Vietcong know we mean business is to kill them, cut out their hearts and livers and eat them for dinner." (I was never able to conclusively determine that the latter statement was true.)

I know they were trying to terrify me. Having fortunately acquired some practice in Oriental composure, I responded, "How interesting. Let's have another beer."

For a moment they were silent. When they started to talk again it was to ask me about my family. I asked them about their families. I ordered more beer. These APT members were among the best rice wine drinkers in Go Cong, but beer was more in my sphere, and they were already quite drunk. Finally, they called it quits.

With the Dragon's Children

One of them said, "Ong Gam, I can tell that you're a strong bastard yourself. I'm drunk already, but you're still drinking beer as though there wouldn't be any left in Go Cong tomorrow." Afterward, we all left the tea shop together.

These team members soon spread the word that Ong Gam wasn't so bad after all. Though their commander, Bao, remained very cool toward me for several more months, I soon became friendly with most of the members. They began to invite me to their notorious parties. Such parties were usually held at one of their homes. As they received a very small salary, most of their homes were made of thatch and bamboo with some windows—without glass—cut into the walls. At these parties, rice wine was always served. There would be one or more of several types of hors d'oeuvres: dried squid; pickled pig entrails; duck feet; chicken feet; twenty-five-day-old fertile duck eggs; and coagulated duck's blood smothered with cashew nuts. The regular meal would consist of meat and rice with fish sauce.[32]

De's name rhymes in Vietnamese—*Ong De Ba Xi De* (Mr. Rice Wine). Another thing De was famous for was his ability to identify Vietcong. Only half-joking, people would say, "De is the only Vietnamese we know who can look another Vietnamese straight in the eye and tell whether he's Vietcong or not." In fact, De did know a lot about the special signs and communication symbols used by the Vietcong. Alone of all the APT members, De managed to avoid going out on any operations. He was always left to come and go as he pleased. No one ever bothered him. Nevertheless, he was extremely valuable because of his singular ability to gather information on anything. He was left alone to make himself useful as he saw fit, but even if he didn't see fit, no one, not even Bao, would pressure him on any matter.

The humorous aspect of charging De with providing the dog was that he happened to have a dog himself. De's dog

David J. Garms

followed him everywhere. It was a mean-looking mutt, with its short nose and large mouth and its long tail that would stiffen whenever it spotted something interesting. It resembled a cross between a bulldog and a pointer. De's dog never liked me; every time I came near De it growled and snapped at me. The other APT members liked to tease De about his dog:

"Why do you keep such an ugly-looking dog, De?"

"De, if you don't catch us a dog we will eat yours!"

"Hey, look at this fat dog! Let's eat this dog!"

De couldn't be sure if they were joking or not. He watched his dog closely.[33]

Within a few days, De was able to catch a dog; it could have been any stray. Knowing that some people liked dog meat, Vietnamese who valued their dogs tended to keep them close at home.

The APT dog-roasting party was set. It was scheduled for a Sunday afternoon so that there would be plenty of time for a leisurely feast. One of the team members offered the use of his home. De had been charged with catching the dog, and now he was appointed chef.

On the appointed day I walked into the kitchen to watch the preparations. De, with a huge grin on his face, was busy roasting the dog's legs and thighs. The claws still stuck out from the feet. De informed me, his grin broadening, that the specialty of the day would be dog's head soup. I was certain that he was only joking.

When all the guests had gathered, we sat around a big table to enjoy rice wine and dried squid while De finished cooking the dog. We had had several glasses of rice wine each when De finally came out of the kitchen. With both hands he was carrying a large bowl. Everyone leaned over and peered into the bowl. With a huge grin still on his face, and his eyes gleaming behind the sunglasses, De stood back to watch our reactions.

With the Dragon's Children

The dog's skull was ugly in the bowl. The tongue hung out and the eyes stared. De began to talk about the dog:

"This is the head of a dog. See his teeth?" He pointed to the teeth. "Quite large, aren't they? Lucky we have this dog's head in the bowl so that he cannot bite anyone anymore. Here is the dog's brain." He fondled the skull. "The brain tells the tongue to bark."

At this point, De reached into the bowl, grasped the dog's boney jaws, ground the teeth up and down, and barked, "Arf, arf, grr, grr, arf...!"

We all collapsed in laughter. I was less inclined to laugh, however, when the soup was dished into bowls and I had to begin to eat. I gave thanks to nature for having provided me with a fairly strong stomach.

CHAPTER VI

A Few More Names

By this time, our efforts to improve the center had enjoyed some success, despite constantly being hampered by the difficulty of obtaining supplies. Financial support for the center in all areas—food, clothing, shelter, training materials for the returnees, staff salaries and maintenance of the center—was the responsibility of the Ministry of Chieu Hoi. The United States made its financial and advisory contribution to the program through MACCORDS (Military Assistance Command/Civil Operations Rural Development Support). The difficulties arose in attempting to receive funds already budgeted and in obtaining supplies not included in the regular budget. It was necessary to secure the provincial chief's authorization to receive money and supplies already budgeted. For other necessary supplies we could approach the Americans in the provincial CORDS team. In many cases, I was able to make use of the AIK (Assistance in Kind) Funds. This was a special fund authorized for the use of each provincial advisory team. It provided for the support of projects which could promise to have an immediate impact. To some degree it circumvented

With the Dragon's Children

the problem of having to wait a year or more for money to be budgeted for a project through ordinary channels.

Trieu quickly proved himself to be very dextrous in extracting assistance from all quarters. The province chief, with his own man installed in the center, became more cooperative than he had been previously in releasing funds authorized by the ministry. We could not generally count on regularly receiving funds for at least staff salaries and for necessities for the returnees.

Trieu and I were both anxious to improve the physical conditions at the center. In particular, Trieu was concerned with making the center's defense perimeter somewhat more formidable than a backyard fence. In its present state, the barrier would not have presented the least obstacle to a Vietcong attack. We might as well have stood at the front gate to receive them with welcome offerings. Trieu had friends in the local Regional Force's Supply Company; he managed to extract some barbed wire and steel fence stakes from them, and the defense barrier was quickly improved.

I too got actively involved in locating materials and funds. I tapped the AIK Fund and secured money to buy paint. The returnees quickly got to work painting all the buildings in the center. With the last of the paint they repainted the long-faded slogans that adorned the tin-sided buildings. Among these were: *Chieu Hoi la sinh lo* (Chieu Hoi is life); *Chieu Hoi la yeu nuoc* (Chieu Hoi is to love your nation); and *Chieu Hoi la ve gia dinh* (Chieu Hoi is to come back to your family).

With the improvement in living conditions and vocational training, the returnees' spirits took a noticeable upswing. It became common to see them smile, and the returnees willingly formed work teams to carry out the improvements. These work teams were organized and led by Pham Van Noi, the administrative manager of the center.

David J. Garms

Noi (pronounced to rhyme with *toy*) had served in the military for twenty years before joining the Chieu Hoi staff. He was just a little guy, short even for a Vietnamese, but he more than made up for it with his aggressive manner and belligerent voice. Noi had a mean bark, but underneath it his heart was gold. He rarely let his heart show because it was his philosophy that "there must be discipline at the Chieu Hoi Center." Noi was tough, but also responsive and concerned. He easily commanded respect from the returnees, and there was never a moment of doubt in their minds that he was a man to be obeyed. He loved action and prided himself on how fast he could get things done, especially in the construction of buildings; he would have been fully at ease with the most aggressive construction foremen in the United States. He also had the ability to relate very well to the poor, perhaps because he himself had come from very humble beginnings. He pointed out his birthplace to me one day as we were driving by: Noi had been born in the rice paddies, just like most of the returnees.

It was amazing to observe how, under Noi's direction, the returnees could be inspired to clean up the center, put up barriers around the compound, construct new buildings, and perform any other labor. He would strut around stiff-backed, shouting orders at as many as seventy of the returnees at a time. Remarkably, the returnees responded to the little man's manner and even appeared to enjoy it. They would smile and giggle and then work even harder.

Noi illustrated his doctrine of strict discipline on a number of occasions. One time, two returnees were fighting on the raised dirt bank that separated two of the fishponds. Noi caught sight of them and ran toward the grappling men. He grabbed one returnee by the collar and threw him into the pond. He thoroughly slapped the other returnee. The fight was stopped cold.

With the Dragon's Children

On another occasion, the returnees had been complaining that they didn't have enough drinking water. Noi hitched up the water tank trailer to the Chieu Hoi jeep and drove off to the water reservoir in the center of town. He filled the water tank and was soon barreling back to the compound with water splashing all over. As he approached the gate he braked the jeep fast. One front wheel slid and knocked stones into the compound. (The jeep, one of two World War II vintage Willys assigned to the center, had already seen one war too many.) When the jeep came to a sliding, scrambling halt, water sloshed back and forth in the tank and gushed out over the top.

Noi jumped from the jeep and came into the office. For several minutes he occupied himself with some papers. Then he glanced out the window and noticed that no one had removed the water from the trailer and put it into the center's cement reservoir.

He let out a scream. "What the hell is going on? The returnees complain that they don't have water and then they don't even empty the tank when I bring it to them. Those lazy bastards!"

He leaped from his desk, ran out of the office, and ordered all the returnees to line up in formation on the volleyball court. Returnees came scrambling from every direction to try to get into some kind of formation. They had never seen Noi so thoroughly mad before. He stood before them with his hands on his hips and his short legs wide apart. The returnees stood stiffly in formation and quaked visibly.

Noi bellowed, "I don't know what you guys think this Chieu Hoi business is anyway—a giveaway program? I don't know what all of you did in the Vietcong ranks, but I'm sure you weren't left to sit around on your asses all day long. Let me now introduce a new concept to you: it's called 'work responsibility.' It is something that you will have to get accustomed

- 85 -

David J. Garms

to, and fast! Do you think that Buddha will put food in your mouth for nothing? No! It doesn't happen to work that way! Work may not be pleasant, but it's very necessary. So, damn it, get to work! Now!"

At his last word, the returnees began to scurry frantically in all directions to find containers to carry the water.

Initially I had thought that Noi's philosophy was a bit harsh, but later I changed my mind completely. The returnees had been heavily regimented in the Vietcong ranks. They were accustomed to strict discipline and would become disoriented in its sudden absence.

A second factor was the age of the returnees. Many of them were under twenty years of age, and a fair number of them were only fourteen, fifteen, or sixteen.[34] These returnees were likely to benefit from regular fatherly discipline. Along with this, Noi also knew how to provide a father's concern. The returnees knew they could confide in him and that he would understand them. Out of his own pocket, he would often buy things for the returnees. He took a special interest in helping them to find jobs once their stay at the center was over. I quickly came to feel the same respect and affection for the blustering little man as did the returnees and staff.

Trieu and Noi were by far the most aggressive staff members at the center. The rest of the staff might have preferred a more relaxed approach to work, but they were quick to recognize the authority—both official and personal—of the two men. Some of the staff were genuinely motivated by the example of Trieu and Noi. Others realized that it simply behooved them to follow suit. Whatever the case, there was a vast improvement in the commitment of everyone to his work.

Major Riddle, the regional Chieu Hoi advisor, came up from Can Tho several times to pay visits to the center. He was impressed.

"I just didn't think it could be done," he said.

With the Dragon's Children

He went on to admit that he had underestimated the potential of the people involved, including me. We were far from being the best Chieu Hoi Center in Vietnam, but we could take pride in the fact that we were no longer the worst.

After Trieu and Noi, the most influential person at the center was Le Ngoc Diep, the man who had given the party my first night in Go Cong. (*Diep* is pronounced as *yip*.) Diep was the district Chieu Hoi chief of Hoa Tan District. A slender young man, he made a fine, even sophisticated appearance. He always came to work in a starched white shirt, pressed trousers, and polished shoes with pointed toes. This might not seem unduly flashy, but at the Chieu Hoi Center in Go Cong it was anything but inconspicuous. The returnees dressed in the traditional Vietnamese shirt and trouser outfit (often called "pajamas" by Westerners). Some of the staff wore the official brown uniform of the Chieu Hoi ministry, but others dressed like the returnees. Except for Diep, the only spots of radiance were provided by the female staff. They dressed in the lovely traditional *ao dai*, a long thin dress slit from the waist to the ankle and worn over loose pants.

Diep had a magician's ability to fit in anywhere. He would have done well even at a high-class cocktail party in the United States. I did, in fact, bring him to some fairly formal cocktail parties in the American community in Saigon. He was not the least bit ill at ease, and it would have been totally inappropriate for anyone to have displayed the slightest degree of condescension toward him. I never did understand where Diep acquired his style. He was the son of a poor carpenter. His formal schooling ended before the eighth grade, and he never did learn English. His intelligence would have allowed him to master English in a short time, but he never made the attempt because of his often stated belief that speaking English would "damage his throat."

David J. Garms

Unlike Noi, Diep was quiet and unobtrusive, and he played all his cards with extreme care. He was a subtle manipulator of people and situations. He was not a man who would ever find himself in the position of having bet on a losing team. I quickly came to recognize and admire Diep's cleverness, and I also came to like the man. Different though Trieu and Diep were in character and manner, they were equally my friends.

The ever-smiling Diep was a gifted administrator and leader. He was also a brilliant self-taught mechanic, electrician, and general handyman. He could do the most amazing things with just an old screwdriver and a pair of bent pliers. The Chieu Hoi Center would have suffered badly without him. Before starting to fix something at the center, Diep would carefully remove his white shirt, pressed pants, and polished shoes. With only his underwear in place, Diep would take his little bag of tools and proceed to fix whatever required his ministrations—the jeeps, generators, doors, windows, or anything else. When he finished his repairs he would put his clothes back on and return to the office, the same starched and pressed young gentleman.

One of Diep's most vital responsibilities was to keep the two Chieu Hoi jeeps running. They were always breaking down, and one day it appeared that one of them was lost for good. Everyone gave up on it except Diep. He decided to remove the engine, and he recruited five returnees to help him. They all stripped down to their underwear. Diep obtained a rope and a six-foot log. The rope was wrapped around the engine and tied firmly to the log. Diep and two of the returnees positioned themselves at one side of the jeep and the three others took up stations on the other side. By this time a crowd had begun to gather. Diep ordered the returnees to grasp the log and prepare to lift the engine at the count of three.

The returnees waited. The crowd waited.

Then came the words, *"Mot! Hai! Ba!"* (One, two, three!)

- 88 -

With the Dragon's Children

Slowly the engine began to rise. The returnees groaned and swore.

Diep shouted, "Lift! Lift!"

The engine was heavier than Diep thought possible but it was now free from the body. Inch by inch the returnees carried it away from the jeep. Slowly, very slowly, it was set on the ground. The crowd cheered. The returnees, red-faced and groaning, sat down, panting heavily.

Diep took some tools from his little bag and got to work. Within a few hours the engine was entirely disassembled. Diep finally determined that the difficulty was caused by the crankshaft bearing having been totally ruined and the crankshaft itself damaged. He explained that, though he could get a new bearing in Go Cong, it would take too long and cost too much to go to Saigon for a new crankshaft. The engine would simply have to get along with the old damaged crankshaft.

"In Vietnam we must rely on individual creativity and luck to keep things going," he said.

Diep installed new bearings on the old crankshaft and put the engine back together. Again he wrapped the rope around the engine and tied it to the log. He called the original six returnees plus two more, and again they strained to lift the engine. Slowly it was raised from the ground, inched over to the jeep, and put back in place. Diep bolted the engine down, put oil in the crankcase, got back into his clothes, started up the engine, and drove down the road. Not only did the jeep run that day, but it ran as long as I was in Go Cong. Luck was indeed with Diep.

On another occasion, Diep's ingenuity was needed to organize a lighting system for the center. As we had only two very dim bulbs connected to the town's power system, I had requested a ten-kilowatt generator from the versatile U.S. Army Excess Property Disposal Depot on the outskirts of Saigon.

David J. Garms

Our excitement over the generator evaporated when it arrived. It was a shambles. (Most of the excess property at the disposal depot was there, of course, because it was usually inoperable.) Our hopes were raised again when Diep promised to try to do something with it. We should never have doubted, for a few days later the center had its own electric system.

However, as I walked by the center one night, I noticed that the lights were very dim. I went to the generator room, saw that the generator engine was running very slowly, and turned up the throttle a bit. Immediately sparks flew all over the center. In the lecture room some banners with slogans on them burst into flames. A moment later the center was in total darkness. After helping to put out the flames, I found myself confronted by a surprisingly contained Diep. He explained to me that, as most of the buildings had no wiring for lights, he had rigged a wiring system out of old telephone wires. These wires could not withstand a high current.

Diep brushed aside my apologies. "Please just don't do this again," he said, and immediately went to get his tools to repair the damage.

Diep's lack of more sophisticated tools handicapped him in the major repair jobs he attempted. We often wondered how we might get better tools for him. There were two Koreans in Go Cong—Kim and You—who worked for an American company called Pacific Architects and Engineers. As they were responsible for repairs throughout U.S. installations in Go Cong, they had been supplied with excellent tools. I sometimes asked the Koreans to help us fix things at the center. Diep would always stare hungrily at their high-quality equipment. He wanted so much just to touch the tools, to see how they might feel in his hands.

The Koreans watched their tools very closely. There were no others like them in Go Cong. I asked the Koreans once if they might consider loaning us the tools. They refused

With the Dragon's Children

delicately, saying, "You know, these tools are hard to get, and if we lost any, it would take weeks or even months before they could be replaced. In the meantime, we have lots of work to do."

I was disappointed, but I could understand their reasoning.

As I came to know the Koreans better, I realized that they had some specific needs too. Kim and You, if given half a chance, were quite friendly young men, but as the only Koreans in the province, they had a difficult time fitting into the provincial advisory team. They had quarters in the MACV compound, and though they lived and worked with Americans, they seemed to have found no friends among them. You knew almost no English and Kim's English was limited. Kim and You must have been lonely, but they never complained, and they always did what was required of them.

I kept wondering if the needs and interests of the Koreans and those of the center might be met to the mutual benefit of everyone. I discussed this with Trieu, and we decided to invite Kim and You to the parties which were held several times a week at the center. At these informal parties, rice wine or beer would be served, and there would be a little something to eat, such as duck feet or pig entrails. Each person would contribute a small sum for the purchase of the refreshments. These parties were not only enjoyable, but they were also very useful. Everyone loosened up, and there was a free exchange of feelings and ideas. Differences were aired, proposals heard, and plans made.

Surprisingly, language never seemed to be a problem. It seemed that if one wanted to communicate then one could. And sometimes more was accomplished during one of these parties than during an entire working day. In view of the latter, I think the parties were often by design, an attempt to accomplish something that couldn't be accomplished in the

David J. Garms

office. Occasionally, I invited one or two other Americans to attend a party, but usually I was the only one present.

Kim and You began to come to some of the parties. Despite a severe language barrier, they seemed to genuinely enjoy them. Their prior reservations about associating with former Vietcong dissipated, and they became quite amiable toward the staff and returnees. At one of the parties, Kim expressed an interest in improving his English, and I promptly offered to tutor him. After several lessons we were quite good friends. One day I approached him again on the subject of the tools. I said, "I see that you are very busy trying to keep up with your regular work. Sometimes I've even seen you working late at night. I hate to ask you to help us out at the center in addition to all your other work. I think that, if you could let us borrow your tools, we could manage by ourselves. I promise to immediately reimburse you for any tools that might be lost." Kim agreed to let us use his tools when he didn't need them.

Diep and Trieu were ecstatic when I told them of Kim's decision. Diep was frantic to get his hands on the tools. I mentioned to him that I had promised Kim to pay for any missing tools. Diep said, "We are all friends at the Chieu Hoi Center. No one would dare to steal anything from anyone else." Despite his protestations, I fully expected some of the tools to disappear. I had misjudged the staff and returnees, however, for I never had to replace a single tool.

The Koreans not only lent us their tools but, before they left Go Cong, they built a Ping Pong table for the returnees. It was the handsomest Ping Pong table ever seen in Go Cong, and it was still being used by returnees several years afterwards. (Before Kim left Vietnam I took him to Can Tho. Another colleague, George Belcher, and I decided to invite Kim out for dinner one night. We went to an "American-managed" restaurant. After we sat down we were asked to leave. We asked why and were advised that Kim couldn't be in the restaurant. How

With the Dragon's Children

embarrassing! George and I protested vehemently but the restaurant manager wouldn't budge. We decided to leave and went to a Vietnamese restaurant where we were all welcome.)

One of the most interesting characters at the center was Sergeant Nguyen Van Ba. He was detailed to the Chieu Hoi Center from the provincial S-2 office. This innocuous-sounding office was, in fact, the intelligence collection and analysis entity for Go Cong. The office was located in a single tin shed about ten by twenty feet. There were a few file cabinets inside and some maps of the province on the walls. Ba was in charge of interviewing all new returnees for possible information on Vietcong locations and activities and then relaying this information to the S-2 office.

No man could have appeared to be less of an intelligence officer than Sergeant Ba. He was forty-five years old, but he looked more than sixty. He was extremely thin, and when asked why this was so he would reply, "Because I drink like hell, chase wild women, and fight Vietcong!" The first was only a minor exaggeration, for Ba was one of Go Cong's most proficient rice wine drinkers, surpassed probably only by De. The third was equally true, for Ba volunteered to go on a number of military operations, and his exploits during them impressed even the APT members. It was the second activity, however, at which Ba truly excelled. He almost lost his job one day when, after one of his monumental drinking bouts, he grabbed the breast of a young, attractive policewoman who was passing by the Chieu Hoi Center. It took Ba several attempts to resolve the sexual harassment activity. Reportedly, the policewoman made Ba suffer big time. She apparently threatened to go to court but then finally agreed to a financial settlement.

Ba, like some other men in Go Cong, kept two wives. It was not uncommon for a Vietnamese male to have both a *ba sa lon* (big wife) and a *ba sa nho* (small wife). Legally, there could only be one wife, but the police didn't prove to be overly diligent in pursuing offenders; they were too busy with more crucial matters, or possibly they had "small wives" of their own.

There was some protocol involved in having two wives. The "big wife" had to be respected for having been the first. She often became something of a mother to her husband as well as her children, and sometimes even to the "small wife." The "small wife" was usually considerably younger and had been acquired for status. Some of my Vietnamese friends who already had a wife would joke about getting a second one. They would say, "I need to raise a 'small wife.'" Trieu was something of an exception, for he never even joked about acquiring a "small wife." Having two wives appeared to be fully accepted, and the existence of the "small wife" was kept secret in very few cases. The major requirements were that the "big wife" should not be neglected by the husband, and that the husband should be capable of supporting both wives.[35]

Sergeant Ba was criticized by many Vietnamese because he failed to meet the requirements. He neglected his "big wife," giving her little attention and scarcely any money. Forced to support herself, she worked as a maid in the CORDS compound. His "small wife" could not have been more than twenty years old. She gave birth to a son a few weeks after I arrived in Go Cong.[36]

Despite certain habits, Ba was thoroughly competent at his job. The returnees found it easy to talk to him, probably because he looked and acted like a peasant himself. Ba was also an authority on the province—the topography, people, climate, and customs. He gave me much useful information on such things, which I passed on to the U.S. provincial advisory team. Ba was particularly knowledgeable about specific people in the Vietcong, including many of those in the most responsible positions. He was often consulted in the identification of

With the Dragon's Children

captured or killed Vietcong. Ba pointed out that, after all, he had gone to school with many of them.

A man named Duc-Ba was also responsible for gathering information from the returnees. The biographic data he collected from each returnee served as a self-declaration as to who the returnee was. Each returnee had a file which constituted a historical record of what he had done, from his birth till his return to the GVN.

Duc-Ba had been a Vietcong himself for over two years, returning to the GVN via the Chieu Hoi Program in 1965. He never talked about his experiences with the Vietcong, and would never even voluntarily admit that he had been one. Everyone knew his past, but recognizing his sensitivity on the subject, no one questioned him about it.

To a greater degree than probably anyone else, Duc-Ba was the returnees' friend. The returnees brought their grievances, fears, and hopes to him. As a sort of grass-roots troubleshooter for any negative developments in the attitudes of the returnees, he was invaluable to the center. He played his important role most discreetly. He avoided being too closely associated with the rest of the staff and very seldom ate or drank with them. Duc-Ba must have suffered in his self-imposed isolation. His closest associates were ex-Vietcong, but he could never bring himself to admit that they shared a common past.

The deputy Chieu Hoi chief, a young man named Truong Van Nhan, might have been a valuable staff member, but he did not choose to be so. He was more impressed with his title than with the responsibility that rested with it. Nhan struck me as a country boy who had finally made it to the city and landed a good job by being a little bit more devious than anyone else. He wasn't able to forget the struggles he had gone through to reach his present position, and he wasn't about to give up what he had achieved for anything. He was

David J. Garms

consistently polite, and he readily responded to my questions about the program, but I always felt that behind the facade was more duplicity and deep-rooted cynicism than could easily be imagined. One obvious reason for Nhan's attachment to his job was that it carried with it an automatic draft deferment. His unmistakable glee at having a draft deferrable position did not endear him to his contemporaries in uniform.

One of Nhan's primary responsibilities was the supervision of the center's clerical staff, which consisted of two men and seven women. One of the male clerks, Nguyen Duy Cuong, was an ex-Vietcong who had worked with the production and dissemination of Vietcong propaganda. When he returned to the GVN he was put to work at much the same thing. Cuong was in charge of propaganda themes, leaflet production and dissemination, loudspeaker broadcasts on APT operations, and showing films to the returnees at the center. Despite his experience and duties, however, Cuong was easily the most irresponsible of the staff members. He would play tricks on the staff women and would not allow anyone a moment's peace. Cuong was the center's resident buffoon, but though everyone laughed at him, he had no real friends. His behavior may have been the result of his difficult circumstances; with his modest salary Cuong could only afford a one-room shack for his wife and two children.

Tran Van Huan, the other male clerk, was the complete opposite of Cuong. He was responsible and highly motivated. He sat at his desk typing all day, rarely saying anything and never troubling anyone. Huan was young and single, but was so shy that he seemed not to notice girls at all. He had a compulsive need to do everything right. It would hurt him terribly when he made an error in his typing. Erasing the error and typing over it caused him such anguish that he would often type the entire page again. As did most of the Vietnamese on the staff, I looked upon Huan as a younger brother. I always

- 96 -

With the Dragon's Children

treated him with extreme care, and he responded very favorably. He constantly asked me if I needed any typing done in Vietnamese, and he was hurt if I didn't require his services frequently.

Though the clerical staff was technically under the supervision of Nhan, the deputy Chieu Hoi chief, everyone knew that it was really Mrs. Huynh Thi Huong who was in control. She was the oldest member of the clerical staff and also the most experienced. By these factors—and also by the force of her personality—she easily commanded the respect and obedience of the other clerical workers.

Unhappily, Mrs Huong's home life was not as easily managed. Her husband, Mr. Chi,[37] worked at the Ministry of Chieu Hoi in Saigon. She knew as well as everyone else that her husband kept a "small wife" in Saigon. Once she expressed to me her feelings about the situation:

"I'm not happy, but what can I do? Men will always play," she said.

Mrs. Huong was consistently kind and helpful to me. Several times, when Mr. Chi was home from Saigon, she invited me to their house for dinner.

The other women on the staff were young and either single or recently married. They looked so delicate and passive that it was sometimes easy to assume that their character matched their appearance. I quickly realized that very often this was a mistake. On one occasion, Cuong and several other men came into my room in the CORDS compound. Cuong happened to notice the bright, glossy cover of a magazine on a shelf. He picked it up and started to page through it. It was an issue of *Playboy*. Cuong called the others over and soon they were all engrossed in turning the pages and making comments. Cuong asked me for the magazine, and I said he could have it on the condition that he not show it to the ladies at the

David J. Garms

center; I didn't wish to offend their delicate sensibilities, and I also wanted them to retain a somewhat dignified image of me.

Shortly afterward, Cuong and I returned to the office. He strutted dramatically past the women, the magazine folded suspiciously under his arm. The women immediately asked him what it was he was concealing under his arm.

"Oh, nothing," Cuong replied.

As I walked into the office that Trieu and I shared, I could hear the women continuing to press Cuong on the matter. Then there were several minutes of ominous silence. I could guess that Cuong had broken under not too much more pressure and that he was showing the magazine to the women. I heard one of them say (not very softly, either), *"Ong Co Van xau lam!"* ("Mr. Advisor is very bad!")

For the next several days, the women made me suffer; whenever I walked through the office I was subjected to critical comments and nasty stares. However, about a week after the incident, one of the married ladies approached me privately and asked for a copy of the same magazine to give to her husband. A day later, one of the single ladies approached me with the request for a copy for herself!

I realized that I had been wrong again, and that in the case of Vietnamese women, their passive appearance should not be mistaken for how strong they truly are.

For example: Vietnamese men often like to believe that they are entirely in control of family affairs, but that is usually not the case. Vietnamese women are generally in charge of the family budget; they are the ones who often stipulate an allowance for the man. Men generally agree with this as they recognize how important it is to have sufficient funds to raise the children. Further, with the wife managing the family resources, the husband can more easily resist pressures from friends to loan them money.

- 98 -

With the Dragon's Children

One of the women in the office had married a returnee, Nguyen Van Thieu. Thieu had been trained as a medic by the Vietcong, and after completing his re-indoctrination course, he became the staff nurse for the returnees and APT members. He was a happy person and always had a ready smile for everyone. He was constantly teased about his name, which happened to be exactly the same as that of the President of South Vietnam. The returnees would call him "The Vietcong President Thieu." They liked to say, "Go Cong is the real capital of Vietnam and Thieu of Go Cong is the real president." They were joking, but I had already come to realize that such humor often subtly revealed a lack of identification with the national government. Very seldom did I witness an unforced display of allegiance that extended beyond the provincial boundaries. Though the staff medic Thieu had a great deal of hands-on knowledge about the practice of medicine under far-from-ideal conditions, he lacked formal training. He probably never would have received such training had it not been for a man known to the Americans and the Vietnamese alike as Doc Homan.

Doc Homan, a most colorful character with a penchant for irreverent humor, was a U.S. Navy Seabee medic. He had a gravelly voice and a bushy mustache, and he kept his hair trimmed short, almost to the scalp.

He liked working with the Vietnamese, and early in 1968, Doc Homan started working with Thieu. He proposed to buy Thieu various small pieces of medical equipment and to train him in their use if Thieu would assist him when he went into the field with the APT. Thieu could have been required to accompany the APT anyway, but Doc Homan wanted to impress upon him that the supplies and training would not be presented as an outright gift, but were to be earned.

On several occasions, I also accompanied Doc Homan when he went into the field to give medical assistance. Officially I served as interpreter, though Doc Homan was

- 99 -

David J. Garms

not one to permit so minor a thing as a language barrier to prevent his communicating with anyone. It was difficult to say who enjoyed these visits more—Doc Homan or the villagers. After the medical examinations were finished, it was important that we sit down to some serious rice wine drinking with the people of the village. Rice wine was all that the villagers were able to offer even the most distinguished visitor, but Doc Homan received it from their hands with as much gratitude and delight as though he were receiving nectar from the gods. The people of Go Cong were rather impressed with the entire thirteen-member Seabee team. The Seabees, a mobile construction unit of the United States Navy, had been sent to Go Cong to improve the district roads. They became quite friendly with the Chieu Hoi staff soon after their arrival. Trieu shrewdly recognized that the Seabees could do a lot to assist the province, and he was also impressed by their possession of bulldozers and other construction equipment never before seen in Go Cong.

Trieu was the first Vietnamese to invite the Seabees over for a get-acquainted party. During the course of the party, the subject of how the Seabees and the Chieu Hoi Center might help each other was introduced. Trieu wanted the rear section of the compound excavated and an embankment built up to serve as an additional defense perimeter. The Seabees were anxious to start construction on living quarters for themselves. Would the Seabees accept bricks, which the returnees could make from a hand-press machine, for the construction of their living quarters in return for using their heavy equipment to excavate the compound?

Yes, they most certainly would. Within a few days of the party, the Seabees had their bricks and the center had its new defense perimeter. Noi was in charge of managing the production of the bricks. Most of the returnees had never made bricks before, but they learned fast and well under Noi's supervision.

- 100 -

With the Dragon's Children

In addition, the returnees could volunteer during their free time to help with the actual construction of the Seabees' quarters and receive eighty piasters (about sixty cents) a day for their work. Another benefit of the entire project, foreseen by Trieu, was that the returnees would acquire valuable new skills by working with the Seabees.

However, all did not go well during the Seabee's use of a dozer to create an earthen barrier around the center. Some graves were disturbed. Trieu went into a state of great despair and agony.

"How should this grave disturbance issue be addressed?" he asked.

Eventually, Trieu went to consult with Minh, his favorite Buddhist monk. Minh decided that an elaborate spiritual ceremony was required to oversee a re-interment of the coffins.

The relationship that developed between the Seabees and the returnees was very warm. These Americans who prided themselves on being tough and ready to take chances were not about to admit to any fears over associating with former Vietcong. In return, the former Vietcong themselves were overwhelmed by the acceptance shown them by these big foreigners. The Seabees and the returnees might once have easily killed each other, but now they just as easily became friends.

The Seabees became equally friendly with some of the APT members. It had taken me months to establish a rapport with the APT, but the Seabees accomplished it in a matter of weeks. One APT member, known simply as Seia (not a typical Vietnamese name), became particularly close to the Seabees. Seia was short and thin and had freckles, the only Vietnamese I ever saw who had them. His movements were fast and restless and he gestured constantly. Though he understood no English at all, Seia seemed to genuinely like Americans. It

David J. Garms

was a habit of his to impersonate any American he happened to meet. Though scarcely flattered, the Seabees were heartily amused by Seia's vivid impersonations of themselves.

Seia's official job was to issue weapons and ammunition to the APT. If any APT members expended ammunition needlessly, such as shooting into the air during Tet (the lunar New Year), Seia would first accord them a severe verbal lashing. Then he would issue them more ammunition. Problems of this nature were not limited to the APT; in many instances the local militia carelessly shot up all their ammunition, with the result that they didn't always have enough to enable them to go out on operations.

Some of the Seabees began coming to the center at night to participate in the informal parties. One of the Seabees, known as Shakey, dropped by the center to visit the returnees virtually every night. He would play volleyball and drink rice wine with them. Shakey had a lot of friends among the returnees, but his favorite was a tall, husky Vietnamese named Buon. One day Shakey said to me, "Buon is a strong guy and I want him to work with us. I want to teach him everything I know." I reminded Shakey that, as Buon had been at the center only a short time, it would be difficult to secure his release, but I promised that I would try.

I arranged for a meeting with Trieu, Noi, Duc-Ba, Shakey, Buon, and myself. I said, "Shakey is a skilled carpenter and mason. He looks upon Buon as a younger brother, and he wants to teach him his skills. Is there any possibility for Buon's early release?"

Trieu listened intently and then turned to Buon. "Do you want to work with this American?"

Buon cleared his throat and replied, "Yes, I want to very much."

Trieu then glanced at Noi and Duc-Ba, who quietly nodded. Trieu turned back to Buon and spoke briskly. "Fine.

With the Dragon's Children

I'll have your release papers made up this afternoon and you can go with him tomorrow."

The decision worked out very well. Shakey said, "I'm going to make a tough Seabee out of this guy."

I had to laugh when I next saw Buon. His sponsor had given him an old pair of boots that were two sizes too large and a pair of old blue jeans. Shakey also required that Buon work with his shirt off like the other Seabees, something that most Vietnamese regarded as very undignified. Buon was terribly anxious to please Shakey, however, and so he quickly adopted all the characteristics mandatory for a true Seabee. He learned to push a wheelbarrow full of cement as fast as any of them, and he could even balance it going up a steep plank.

Shakey was terribly proud of his protégé and boasted to everyone of each new accomplishment. Buon was happy, and he was also learning many skills. The relationship between the burly American and the ex-Vietcong seemed almost too good to be true; perhaps that was why it wouldn't last.

Shakey surpassed every other Seabee in drinking, causing him increasing difficulties with his OIC (officer-in-charge). Early one morning, I was driving my jeep (which had been assigned to me by CORDS) to the CORDS compound when I saw Shakey staggering down the road in the direction of the Chieu Hoi Center. I stopped the jeep as he approached.

He pounded his fist on the hood of the jeep and shouted, "Goddamn it, Garms, what the hell are you doing this morning?"

"Nothing much," I replied.

"Well, how about giving me a ride to the Chieu Hoi Center where my friends are?"

I agreed to give him a lift if he would promise not to cause any trouble.

"Shit, I won't cause any trouble," he replied as he jumped in.

- 103 -

David J. Garms

I turned the jeep around in the middle of the road and headed back to the center. Shakey asked to be let off in front of Mr. Uncle's tea shop. As he got out he said, "Thanks. I'm going to get so drunk on rice wine that I won't be able to see straight. My friends are here, not in the American compound."

"Don't cause any trouble now," I repeated.

"Hell no," said Shakey. "These people are my friends."

"Okay," I said. "I'm going to the CORDS office. I should be back in an hour."

It was almost two hours before I finally got back to the Chieu Hoi Center. I stopped in first at Mr. Uncle's tea shop. Shakey was still there, and he had gathered quite a crowd around him. There was one elderly Vietnamese gentleman who was addressing Shakey in French. Shakey didn't understand French any more than he did Vietnamese, but that didn't deter him in the least. The old gentleman would say something in French and Shakey would reply, "Yes, you're right. I agree with that a hundred percent." The old gentleman would then continue in French. As everybody seemed to be having a good time, I left Shakey to himself and his friends and went back to work.

Trieu and I had been working on some administrative matters for about an hour when we heard Shakey's voice coming from the clerical section of the office.

"How are all you sweeties today?" he asked the secretaries.

The women hadn't the slightest idea what he was saying. They just giggled.

I went into the clerical section, took Shakey by the arm, and led him into the office I shared with Trieu.

Shakey saluted Trieu. "How the hell are you today, Lieutenant?" he said. Then he turned to me. "I'm really rotten drunk. I can't possibly go back to work like this. Do you have any place where I can sleep this off?"

- 104 -

With the Dragon's Children

I looked at Trieu. "Take him to the bunker at the back of the compound," he said.

I led Shakey to the bunker while the returnees scrounged up a bamboo mat and a pillow. It was the best they could do for their friend. Shakey promptly dozed off to sleep.

Later in the afternoon, a member of the Seabee team who had come to collect some bricks spotted Shakey fast asleep in the bunker. The Seabee left the bricks and hurried off to report to the OIC. The OIC stormed into the center and pulled Shakey out of the bunker. Shakey was transferred out of Go Cong that same evening. The returnees were despondent for days afterward. Buon quit working with the Seabees and came back to the center, but as long as he remained there he never stopped talking about his buddy.

Within several months of my arrival in Go Cong, I had become familiar with district as well as province officials. As indicated earlier, there were four districts in the province: Hoa Tan, Hoa Lac, Hoa Binh, and Hoa Dong. Each district had its own district chief, and most public services, such as public health, public works, and police are represented at the district level.

The Chieu Hoi Program was represented in each district by a district Chieu Hoi chief, though not by a separate physical center. A district Chieu Hoi chief was responsible for receiving new returnees and bringing them to the provincial center, and for keeping track of the status and welfare of returnees who had completed the re-indoctrination course and had settled in his district.

Except for Diep, all of Go Cong's district Chieu Hoi chiefs were themselves former Vietcong. Diep was the Chieu Hoi chief of Hoa Tan District in addition to his responsibilities at the center. Dao Minh Sang, Chieu Hoi chief of Hoa Lac

District, was very popular both with the Vietnamese and with the American advisors of his district.

Nguyen Van Bieu, Chieu Hoi chief of Hoa Binh District, had once been the APT company commander for the province, but he had been removed from the latter position by the province chief and replaced with Bao. As Chieu Hoi chief of Hoa Binh, Bieu's problems were many. Hoa Binh was located in the forested area of southern Go Cong, and these forests had traditionally been the stronghold of the Vietcong in the province.

In addition, the district chief of Hoa Binh did not support the Chieu Hoi Program, and he was also a most difficult man to get along with. Trieu once said of him, "He is not a good man. In addition, he doesn't know how to be polite." The distinction that Trieu made between a man being "good" and being "polite" was typically Vietnamese, for the Vietnamese placed a high premium on outward congeniality, regardless of what his inner nature might be. The Vietnamese would go to all extremes to avoid a head-on confrontation, except on the battlefield. Many times, when an argument was looming among staff members at the center, someone would suddenly say, "Forget it. Let's go have a beer." The conflict would not be solved in this way, of course, but when the people involved returned to it they would do so in a calm, reasonable state of mind rather than in the heat of emotion. I grew to appreciate this attitude toward personal conflicts.

Of the three district Chieu Hoi chiefs who had themselves been Vietcong, it was Nguyen Minh Khiet of Hoa Dong who most engaged my interest. (*Khiet* can be pronounced as the two English words *key it*.) Khiet had not only been a Vietcong, he had been an important one. He had held the post of Vietcong intelligence officer for Hoa Dong. After his return to the GVN in 1965,[38] he went back to Hoa Dong to become the

With the Dragon's Children

Chieu Hoi chief of the same district in which, months before, he had been one of the most influential Vietcong.

Khiet's case was not at all that of a young, uneducated peasant who became a Vietcong under duress, or because he thought it would be an exciting thing to do: Khiet had been a believer. He had joined the Vietminh as a young man, and later became a Vietcong during the Diem regime.

Khiet was not only well-educated, he was also one of the most highly intelligent Vietnamese I ever met. My curiosity had been aroused by this man even before I met him. The first time I came face to face with the tall man with the quiet eyes, I found myself somewhat disturbed. The typical Vietcong returned to the GVN because he was weary of fighting and hiding and because he didn't want to be killed. The GVN might honestly promise such a man that he wouldn't have to fight and hide, and would assure him that his chances for staying alive would be somewhat greater. A man like Khiet, though, would not weary of fighting for his beliefs and could not be moved by fear. To Khiet and those like him, the GVN had to make promises of a different nature. After meeting Khiet, I felt that those promises were extremely important to keep.

Khiet had become a returnee because of his disillusionment with the Vietcong cause. He could not see that the rule the Vietcong exercised over a village by night was more benevolent than that exercised in daylight by the GVN. He resented his loss of personal freedom in the highly regimented Vietcong organization. Elections in the GVN might leave a good deal to be desired, but there were no elections at all among the Vietcong. (However, I was advised that elections did take place at the hamlet level.) He could not see that the Vietcong were truly winning the people, nor could he see that they were winning the war. Khiet had believed and served and waited, but the promises were not being kept. Finally, he changed his

- 107 -

David J. Garms

allegiance, and it was for the other side now that he believed, and served, and waited.

As district Chieu Hoi chief of Hoa Dong, Khiet quickly won the respect and trust of everyone. He was enormously competent and dedicated. A man of profound self-control, he expended little of his time and energy on the diversions so beloved by many of the people of Go Cong. Officially he was the district Chieu Hoi chief of Hoa Dong. Unofficially he also served as the district chief's personal political advisor and intelligence collector. Early in 1968, Khiet was promoted to the post of deputy Chieu Hoi chief of the province. Then he commanded the ear of the province chief himself on matters of politics and intelligence.

In Go Cong it was possible for an ex-Vietcong of Khiet's ability to achieve a position of authority. In other provinces where the fighting had been more fierce and the feelings more bitter, this was rarely possible. A man who had attained a high military or political rank with the Vietcong might hesitate, even after becoming disillusioned with the Vietcong cause, to declare himself with the GVN if he thought that all that awaited him was the option to become a peasant working a few rented acres, or a private drilling in the local militia.

Recognizing this, and anxious to attract men from the highest ranks in the Vietcong, the GVN came out with the National Reconciliation Program in 1967. The crux of this program was that a returnee would be given a position roughly equivalent to that which he had held in the Vietcong. A medic with the Vietcong could become a medic in the GVN. A Vietcong lieutenant could expect to become a lieutenant in ARVN or the Regional Forces. Following the implementation of the program, the number of high-ranking returnees did, in fact, increase. However, it would be difficult to say to what extent this was a direct result of the program rather than the result of a combination of other factors.

- 108 -

With the Dragon's Children

Khiet and I had many discussions on the merits and defects of the Chieu Hoi Program. He, along with several other officials connected with the center in Go Cong, stressed not its much-vaunted value in depleting Vietcong ranks and bringing to the GVN men, weapons, and intelligence so much as its essentially humanitarian aspect.

"It used to be that, once a man chose to join the Vietcong, he had no more choices," Khiet told me. "With the Chieu Hoi Program, he still had a choice, for he can remain a Vietcong or he can return to the GVN. Two choices are not many, though it is better than one."

Both the GVN and U.S. authorities liked to point out that, while it cost thousands of dollars to bring about the death of a single Vietcong,[39] it cost only about $300 to make him a returnee. Khiet and some others would comment that, money aside, each returnee was one more life spared.[40] Of course, it was difficult to predict how this life that had been spared might be used. Each returnee who completed his re-indoctrination and walked out of the center a free man might be an asset to the GVN, or he might one day fight again in the ranks of the Vietcong.

Whatever he might become, he would be a living person for at least a little while longer, and while he lived he would be a participant in deciding the fate—whatever that fate might be—of his village, his district, his province, and his country.

CHAPTER VII

Presenting Mr. Cat

By October, everyone connected with the Chieu Hoi Center had some cause to be proud of what had been accomplished. The province chief did not conceal his displeasure over the evidence that the Chieu Hoi Center was able to continue and even to grow without his approval and support. There were some who, understandably, took pleasure in the province chief's displeasure, particularly when the center became known as one of the real successes, not only in the province, but in the region. The province chief could hardly share any of the credit for this as his opposition to the Chieu Hoi Program was well known.

As a sign of its disapproval of the province chief's abrupt dismissal of the previous Chieu Hoi chief, the Ministry of Chieu Hoi had refused to appoint a replacement. As indicated earlier, the province chief's retaliation had been to appoint Trieu as the acting chief. This was how matters had rested for several months. We had all begun to hope that this particular war, at least, was over.

With the Dragon's Children

It was not to be so, for suddenly the ministry returned to the field and resumed the struggle. One afternoon in early October, I looked out from the office to see Trieu escorting an elderly gentleman into the compound. I stared: a suit and tie, polished shoes, French-style spectacles, and gold cuff links were not common in Go Cong. I went forward to meet them, and a moment later Trieu was introducing me to the new Chieu Hoi chief. His name was Vo Van Cat, and I was most unimpressed. (*Cat* should be pronounced like the English word *cot*.)

The ministry had not troubled itself to inform any of us that a new chief was on the way, but in any case we would not have expected to receive an elderly Saigon bureaucrat. I was deeply disappointed. *Things have been going so well, and Trieu and I have established such a fine working relationship.* I thought. *Now I'll have to start out all over again with a person who knows nothing about Go Cong, the Chieu Hoi staff, or what we've been doing here.*

Prior to turning the center over to Mr. Cat, Trieu spent several days briefing him. There were inventories, accounts, memos, and introductions to be taken care of. I used this interval to try to discover what had happened in the ministry to bring Mr. Cat down upon us. I sent a memorandum to Major Riddle pointing out that abrupt changes in personnel could severely curtail the momentum that the program had gained. Trieu, Diep, Noi, and Khiet had started something valuable and so unique and fragile that it was easily endangered.

After waiting a week without hearing from Major Riddle, I decided to go to him myself. When I reached Can Tho I discovered that neither Major Riddle nor his Vietnamese counterpart, Colonel Thuc, understood the ministry's move, and that both of them were anxious that Trieu become the permanent Chieu Hoi chief. Colonel Thuc said that he was going to Saigon

- 111 -

David J. Garms

in a few days, and he promised to personally take the matter up with the ministry.

Shortly afterward, Major Riddle came to Go Cong to pay a visit to the province chief. Major Riddle reminded Thuc that he had been able to remove Trieu's predecessor, and he should therefore be able to do something about his successor as well.

The province chief certainly didn't need any encouragement. He was not at all interested in having Saigon succeed in placing one of their own men, a man who wouldn't feel constrained to display much loyalty to his province chief. He indicated that he fully intended to take action immediately.

While waiting to learn what would happen next, I decided I might as well try to get along with Mr. Cat. This was profoundly difficult. I learned that he was only in his late forties, but he seemed like a very old man already. I didn't think it would be likely that he would ever come up with anything innovative or exciting. He sat at his desk all day and sifted through papers. To his credit, he had mastered the labyrinth of the Vietnamese bureaucracy, but then, he had been a civil servant most of his life. He had begun his acquaintance with paperwork under the French colonial government. He spoke French fluently, but knew no English. Mr. Cat very obviously had no use for me. He seemed to regard the assignment of a young American to be his personal advisor as constituting nothing less than the lowest form of insult. I began to appreciate all the more Trieu's acceptance of me and the relationship which we had been able to establish. The staff and returnees had not been able to discover anything inspiring in their new leader either, and morale began to sag badly.

When a month had passed since Mr. Cat's entrance, I realized that nothing was going to be done about removing him. I didn't know (and never would) what Colonel Thuc and the province chief had attempted to do, but their plans had obviously failed. I found myself wondering whether things

- 112 -

With the Dragon's Children

might not have turned out better had Major Riddle and I, as foreigners, not attempted to intervene. Colonel Thuc, the province chief, and the ministry were playing something of a game, and this was a game that no outsider could really fathom. It was their game and they made the rules, and it was obvious that no matter how we might advise them, in the end it was still going to be their game.

Major Riddle suggested that I transfer to another province, but I was already committed to many things in Go Cong. This left me with the single option of trying to get along with Mr. Cat to whatever degree the impossible might prove to be possible. We managed to carry out routine matters, but on any major issue it was certain that we would disagree. It was Mr. Cat's philosophy that administrative matters should always be taken care of first. As so many things demanded attention, it was necessary to establish priorities, and to his mind paperwork should be accorded first priority.

To add to all other problems at this time was my growing concern over Trieu's health. For two weeks prior to Mr. Cat's arrival, Trieu had been gradually succumbing to some strange malady. I had taken him to the local hospital where he was examined both by locally trained Vietnamese doctors and by members of the Spanish medical team.[41] He was given some medicine and sent home. When he failed to get better, I asked a U.S. Army medic, Sergeant Barker, to examine him. The medic declared that Trieu was seriously dehydrated and required intravenous feeding immediately. He was given intravenous feeding for one night, and though he felt somewhat better the next day, I could not fathom why he refused to allow the medic to examine him again. Shortly after Mr. Cat's arrival, Trieu asked me to drive him into town to be examined by a Vietnamese doctor who had been trained in France. He was examined, given some more medicine, and sent home.

David J. Garms

His condition continued to deteriorate. I began making plans with the U.S. medical unit stationed in Go Cong to have Trieu evacuated immediately by helicopter to the nearest U.S. Army hospital. The plans had to be abandoned when I asked Trieu if he would permit us to take him to the hospital; he'd responded with an emphatic "No."

I was frantic; concerned that he might die, I left him that day, afraid that he might not live through the night. When I returned the following day, his wife invited me to his bedside. I was surprised to see an old Chinese doctor crouching over Trieu, making tiny cuts across his forehead. Blood was already dripping from the cuts.

If Trieu isn't doomed already, he'll surely die now from shock and loss of blood, I thought.

Trieu obviously had called in the old Chinese doctor, however, and therefore I didn't try to intervene.

When I returned the following morning I found Trieu sitting up in bed, feeling better than he had in weeks. Trieu smiled at me, for he knew that I would never willingly have permitted the Chinese doctor to treat him. I would never know if Trieu's improvement was due to the Chinese doctor, or to the cumulative effect of all the treatments he had received, or if it had occurred spontaneously, but two weeks later Trieu was on his feet again.

With my worry over Trieu's health relieved, I could devote my full attention to the attempt to learn to work with Mr. Cat. As a last-ditch effort, I invited him over for dinner. We had a rather relaxed meal which grew progressively more relaxed with the consumption of several beers. We talked about various aspects of the war, and Mr. Cat pointed out that he had known virtually continuous war for most of his adult life. When I asked about his family, Mr. Cat suddenly opened up.

With the Dragon's Children

"I do not like to be away from my family," he said, "but it is one of the problems of war. I have worked hard as a civil servant for twenty years, but I have not been able to acquire any security. So many of my friends and relatives have been killed by the French, or the Vietminh, or the Americans, or the Vietcong, or GVN, or sometimes I haven't even known by whom. There is no justice in war, and I want to do something to end it. I am a Buddhist, and I do not feel I can help by killing people. The ministry in Saigon told me that the Chieu Hoi Program in Go Cong needed help. I volunteered to come here because I thought that I could do something in this way."

How unreasonable of me to resent Mr. Cat because he's not another Trieu, I thought. They're different people, having capabilities and interests in different areas. If Mr. Cat volunteered to come to Go Cong, I can certainly try harder to work with him.

"I'm very impressed with your dedication," I said, "and I sympathize with your desire to do something to help end this war. I too have come here voluntarily, and I too want to do something."

Mr. Cat paused a moment, shifted in his chair, and then, in a most polite manner said, "Excuse me, but how do you think you can help me?"

I throttled my suspicions that my worth as an individual was being questioned, and responded, "Each person wants to do well in life. I'm sure that you aspire to better things for yourself and your family. I think that I can assist you. There are ways I can get funds to renovate and expand the center. If you can arrange for the labor and take care of the administrative aspects, I can concentrate on the other things. If the Chieu Hoi Program in Go Cong can be dramatically improved, the ministry will learn what has been done. You will have made an important contribution, and your contribution will not go unnoticed."

David J. Garms

Mr. Cat was deep in thought. "Yes," he murmured, "perhaps something is possible." Then he abruptly excused himself and walked out into the dark street. He was staying at the Buddhist Welfare Center for just a few piasters a day. Home to him in Go Cong was a large room which he shared with several other men.

The next day I arrived at the center earlier than usual. I found Mr. Cat already busy plowing through the usual memoranda. Without pausing to look up, he asked me if I had slept well. He was so engrossed in his papers that I answered only briefly. I went to my desk and started working.

Nearly an hour later Mr. Cat still hadn't spoken further, so I left the office and wandered over to Mr. Uncle's tea shop. I met some APT members there having coffee. We talked a while, and then I went back to the office. Mr. Cat was still busy getting out memos and checking files, and he appeared to take no notice of my return. I hadn't been back at my desk more than a few minutes when he suddenly burst into speech.

"All night I was thinking of ways to improve this center," he said. "We must pick those things which will have the greatest physical and psychological impact. I've just decided that the first thing we must do is to have sidewalks put in. The center will look much better and we won't be walking in mud all the time."

I allowed myself a moment to collect my senses after this onslaught of decisiveness.

"Putting in sidewalks would be an excellent start. I'll try to get 30,000 piasters for the purchase of the materials," I said.

Mr. Cat said he would make the arrangements for the labor. I told him I thought I should be able to get the money in a few days. In fact, I got the money from the AIK Fund the following afternoon. Mr. Cat directed Noi to purchase sand and other materials. Cement was donated by the Provincial Rural Development Office.

With the Dragon's Children

I had thought that, after this burst of activity, Mr. Cat might pause before beginning actual construction of the sidewalks. The morning after I got the money, however, I arrived at the center to discover twenty-five returnees busting up old clay bricks to serve as fill for the sidewalks. Noi was right out there happily ordering the returnees around. Mr. Cat stood nearby issuing orders to Noi. The sidewalks were finished in a week.

Most of the staff thought that Mr. Cat might want to rest on his laurels for a while and return to his neglected paperwork, but a week after the sidewalks were put in he informed me that the next project would be a library.

"A library?" I asked.

"Yes," he said, "I want to build a library for the returnees. I will have all kinds of books placed in it, possibly even some colorful magazines. In addition, I want to have the library built in a traditional Chinese style. It will be a gathering place for friends and relatives who visit the returnees. When it's cool at night, we can all rest after a hard day of work and sit out there drinking beer and discussing the program. Finally, I want the library built near the road so that everyone will see it and know that we are doing things for the returnees."

I agreed that the idea was an excellent one. I tapped the AIK Fund, and this time it yielded 50,000 piasters to cover most of the costs of construction. Again, as soon as I handed over the money, construction began. I was astounded by Mr. Cat's ability, once he had put his papers aside, to become a man of decision and action.

Mr. Cat consulted Noi about the design. They both became very excited, and sometimes Noi would literally shake with enthusiasm. They decided to build the library right in the middle of the fishpond at the front of the center. A footbridge would serve as the approach to the library/teahouse.

David J. Garms

The returnees began construction with the fabrication of four reinforced concrete poles to support the building over the water. Slowly, the library began to take shape, with Noi screaming directions and the returnees scurrying here and there to carry them out.

"Work fast! Fast! Let's get this thing built!" Noi shouted.

The returnees loved it. Noi and the returnees were joined in a common goal which they all wanted equally to achieve. This was something that they were all a part of from the beginning, something which would belong to all of them when it was finished. And it *would* be finished; Noi would see to that. He could scarcely take his eyes off the construction as it progressed.

Sometimes, even early in the morning or late at night, he would walk around the partially-completed structure to kick the floor and push on the pillars. The whole structure was solid enough, but Noi loved testing it anyway. Even Mr. Cat had reached such a pitch of excitement that he could hardly concentrate on his memos anymore. Everyone's attention was focused on the rising structure, not only at the center, but in town, too.

It affected me to see the returnees so involved and happy. They were proud of what they were doing. They needed to believe Noi when he told them, "You should not be ashamed of being a returnee. There have been many good people with the Vietcong. Now we have something special to accomplish here at the center, and you are all a part of it. There is the library to finish first, but we're not going to stop there. We won't stop until we make this the best Chieu Hoi Center in the entire country!"

Mr. Cat was already making plans for the dedication ceremony. It was to be as elaborate as possible. He asked me to invite Major Riddle. Major Riddle couldn't attend, but he promised to send a representative on his behalf.

- 118 -

With the Dragon's Children

Finally, late in November, the great day came. Major Riddle's representative, the province chief, the U.S. province senior advisor, and an assortment of other notables —American and Vietnamese—attended. Mr. Cat was in his element conducting the official tour of the library/teahouse. It was indeed, for Go Cong, a most unique and impressive structure. The floor and walls were made of wood, and the four-sided roof was of tin. A small cement bridge with a wooden handrail stretched twelve feet across the fishpond to the library. Inside, there was a table and benches and bookshelves. There were even windows with screens. The tour was followed by a series of speeches.

After the dedication ceremony was over and the dignitaries had left, Mr. Cat ordered that a case of beer be purchased. Noi insisted on paying for it, and he sent a returnee scurrying off to Mr. Uncle's tea shop. We all then retired to the library/teahouse for an unofficial dedication celebration. After we had all had several beers, Mr. Cat stood up and made an impromptu speech.

With his head up and his thin chest stuck out, he declared, "This Chieu Hoi Center was in the worst possible condition for a long time. We all, returnees and staff, have worked hard to improve it. We have done it ourselves, and we let no one stop us." With tears filling his eyes, and pausing frequently to swallow, he continued. "We must not stop here. We must continue with increased efforts. Two months from now the Go Cong Chieu Hoi Center will be the best in Region IV." He turned to me and nodded. "Please pass this on to Major Riddle," he added. Mr. Cat sat down to a hearty applause.

The following day, Mr. Cat called a meeting of the staff and representatives from the returnees. I think he recognized that he'd had a lot to drink the night before and that he'd made a lot of promises.

David J. Garms

He started off the meeting by saying, "I want to discuss a very important matter with all of you today—the improvement of our center. I sincerely need the help of each and every one of you." Mr. Cat assumed an uncharacteristically humble manner as he spoke; his head was not high now and his speech was not condescending or authoritarian. Everyone listened most intently. Mr. Cat asked for proposals of ways in which the program could be improved. Ideas and suggestions were offered from every part of the room:

"Build signboards with Chieu Hoi slogans on them and put them up all over the province!"

"Improve and expand the recreational facilities!"

"Print more leaflets, pamphlets, and newsletters"

"Improve the defense capabilities of the center!"

"Begin a newspaper!"

The response to Mr. Cat's request for suggestions was overwhelming.

Meanwhile, trouble was brewing with the province chief. He had become increasingly discontented with Mr. Cat's lack of deference toward him, and I had heard rumors that he had started to publicly criticize Mr. Cat. Mr. Cat must have heard the rumors too. He had never openly defied the province chief, but his manner and very presence served the same end.

I began to worry about Mr. Cat's health. He was working far too hard, and though he would never show it, he must have been doing a lot of worrying too. I had come to like and respect the little man, and now I found myself admiring him. I was not the only one who sensed what was happening; it was coming to be known throughout the province that the province chief was not pleased with Mr. Cat.

Naturally there were some people who thought they could take advantage of the situation. Phan Van Chau, the previous Chieu Hoi chief whom the province chief had abruptly removed and replaced with Trieu, had held ideas of getting

- 120 -

With the Dragon's Children

his position back even after Trieu had succeeded him. He had made several trips to Saigon and Can Tho to rally support for his reinstatement.

Mr. Cat made a somewhat easier target than Trieu, and so Chau's hopes had risen. He began to spread bad stories about Mr. Cat whenever he had the chance. He quickly recruited two allies from among Mr. Cat's own staff. Nhan, the deputy Chieu Hoi chief, and Cuong, in charge of propaganda for the program, had not liked Trieu and liked Mr. Cat even less. They preferred an easygoing, permissive chief who would not require too much work of them. Furthermore, they were indebted to Chau, for as Chieu Hoi chief he had gotten them their jobs.

It was reported to me that Nhan and Cuong had received a sum of money from an unknown source in return for informing the local police that Mr. Cat was guilty of extortion and the misuse of government funds. The police reported this to the province chief, and a full investigation of the matter was immediately ordered. As soon as he learned this, Mr. Cat requested the province chief's permission to go to Saigon on Chieu Hoi business, though his real intention was to alert the ministry about the upcoming investigation. The province chief guessed the true nature of the request and refused to give his permission. Mr. Cat decided to leave anyway, and though he tried to leave undetected, someone saw him and reported it to the province chief.

The province chief was further enraged by this latest display of independence. Chau and his followers were delighted that the province chief was so offended. They knew that if Mr. Cat was removed, the province chief might be compelled, for lack of other candidates, to reappoint Chau, particularly if Chau was to show marked loyalty toward the province chief during this difficult time.

David J. Garms

While Mr. Cat was still in Saigon, Chau decided to go drinking one morning. He easily persuaded Nhan and Cuong to join him even though they were supposed to be at work at the center. As Mr. Cat was not expected back that day, they anticipated no difficulties. The trio of conspirators drove off in Chau's French-made car to a bar in another district. (As is partially evident from the Citroen car, Chau had no pressing need to work for money; his concern was in holding a government job that carried with it a draft deferment.)

While Chau, Nhan, and Cuong were gone, Mr. Cat suddenly returned from Saigon. He was furious when he learned how two of his subordinates were passing the workday. He was like an alligator with an abscessed tooth looking for anything on which to take out his rage. Mr. Cat did not have to wait too long for the most appropriate relief.

Late in the afternoon, Nhan and Cuong casually sauntered back to the center. As they were not favorites of the staff, no one bothered to warn them that Mr. Cat had returned and was sitting in his office at that moment, poised for the attack. When Nhan and Cuong walked into the clerical section, Mr. Cat screamed from inside his office, "Hey, you lazy bastards! Get in here immediately!"

Numb, with their faces devoid of everything except fear, they entered the office. Mr. Cat did not ask them to take seats. They had to remain standing as he began to sink his teeth in deeper and deeper.

"I have never seen anyone so irresponsible as you two. You both have good positions, but you have obviously decided to abuse them. People are dying in this war, but you choose to spend it away from your duty, out getting drunk."[42] He glared at them. "I'm disgusted with you two!" After pausing a moment to catch his breath, he directed his next assault at Nhan.

"Nhan, you are the deputy Chieu Hoi chief, but you aren't competent to perform far less than that. Well, you are

- 122 -

With the Dragon's Children

deputy no longer. You are banished to the district until you get your senses back, and if you don't perform well there, we will have no more Mr. Nhan in the Chieu Hoi Program. You will then have to fight Vietcong, and if I have anything to do with it, you will do so in the front lines. Starting immediately you are district Chieu Hoi chief of Hoa Lac. Leave my office!"

Mr. Cat then directed his attention to the quaking Cuong. "You know, Cuong, you have never been of much value. In fact, you have had a distinctly negative effect. I think I will just recommend to Saigon that you be fired. Now, get out of my office so I can get some work done!"

Cuong and Nhan met outside the office and immediately went to find Chau. The three of them had even more motivation for their scheming now. On several occasions they had already asked me what I thought of Mr. Cat, and they had pressed me to divulge the exact sum of money which Mr. Cat had received for the purpose of improving the center. I'd refused to tell them anything. My sympathies were with Mr. Cat, but I was trying extremely hard to be neutral. I had learned from my experience in attempting to influence the original appointment of Mr. Cat that it was far better if the Vietnamese were left alone to settle their own differences. This time I was attempting to exert no influence at all.

As far as whether the allegations against Mr. Cat were true or not was concerned, I was again neutral. I had already seen so much corruption, varying from the petty to the massive, that the whole subject left me rather numb. It was simply the way of life (or, perhaps more accurately, the way of war) in Vietnam. There was nothing that I could do to stop it, and rather than tear my hair out over it, I had some time before deciding simply to ignore it as much as I could. I had made it clear to my co-workers and friends that I did not want to get involved in such activities, and for the most part they respected my wishes and did not press me on the matter.

David J. Garms

Only a dreamer—or a new arrival in Vietnam—would have attempted to grapple with the corruption problem head-on. For years there had been an elaborate system of payoffs. It was an accepted part of the cost of doing such things as starting a business, getting a passport or other legal documents, or obtaining a job. With the influx of American troops and civilians, money, and commodities, the temptations were far greater.

Such temptations tended to generate more envy than gratitude. An ARVN captain might or might not be grateful because there were U.S. troops fighting beside him, but it was inhuman to expect that he would not resent knowing that he, a captain and veteran of ten or more years of service, did not make as much money as one of the American privates.

Furthermore, this was wartime, and the philosophy of many Vietnamese was that they had been presented with opportunities which might not last long, and that they would be fools not to take advantage of them while they could. The effect of being confronted with such wealth was almost hypnotic. My friends in Go Cong tried to explain it to me in these terms: "Americans have so much money. Even if they lose a small portion of it, they will be able to go on. This is not the case with us. We must be very careful. We cannot afford to be unselfish. We do not have the security that you Americans can depend upon. We have only ourselves."

An American friend of mine in Hue, John Roberts, once told me a revealing story. When his transistor radio disappeared he told his Vietnamese students of his regret over losing it. The students tried to cheer him by reminding him that he could easily afford to buy another. The American (who understood the Vietnamese people very well) replied that the radio had been a gift from his parents and that it had a sentimental value that money could not replace. The students could

With the Dragon's Children

understand this and were quite affected by it. A few days later the radio reappeared.

The most obvious example of corruption was, of course, the black market. From the muddy city of Cau Mau in the south to war-ravaged Quang Tri province near the Demilitarized Zone, the black market was widespread and stunningly well-organized. I might go into any of the U.S. military exchanges and still not be able to find what I wanted in liquor, cigarettes, or razor blades, but there was virtually not a single street in any city or town in South Vietnam where I would not be able to buy these things openly, though at several times the military exchange price. These commodities had been imported for the sole and exclusive use of U.S. personnel and Allied Forces; often the price in dollars and cents was still clearly stamped on the items, but some of these items had never even seen the inside of an exchange. I sometimes wondered if the black market was not the single most highly-organized institution in the entire country. One of the best managed entities in South Vietnam was the Saigon Zoo, which had no American advisors.

Americans would often complain of being victims of corruption in Vietnam, but it was difficult to ignore the evidence that some of them were participants as well. From the enlisted man who bought a carton of cigarettes at a military exchange and resold it on the black market, to the high-ranking contract civilian who smuggled in a thousand dollars of U.S. currency and/or gold every time he returned from a trip to Hong Kong, some Americans were indeed participants. The excuses the Americans made (and many would talk about it quite frankly) were most often along the lines of "I didn't ask to be in this godforsaken place. Why shouldn't I try to make a little money? It's easy. Everybody's doing it, so why should I be the only loser?"

I frequently heard U.S. officers complain that their men were learning corruption from the Vietnamese. On the other

- 125 -

David J. Garms

hand, more than one Vietnamese complained to me that their young people were being ruined by the Americans, that the Americans had imported corruption along with tanks and guns. They were incredulous when I tried to explain that there was essentially no black market in the United States and that bribery was not the way of life. The question of who was teaching whom in Vietnam was an impossible one to answer. It might be countered most simply with the observation that war itself is quite a teacher and one that draws many to sit at its feet.

Mr. Cat's attempt to transfer Nhan and fire Cuong had some repercussions. The ministry would not authorize the latter, and Cuong stayed on at the center. Mr. Cat succeeded in having Nhan finally transferred to Hoa Lac District. However, the U.S. advisor to Hoa Lac, an army major, had gotten along with Nhan's predecessor extremely well and was infuriated by the change. He raced in from Hoa Lac and charged into the office, screaming profanities and demanding that his man be returned.

I tried to explain that the change was necessary and that I had concurred with Mr. Cat, but the major ignored me and directed all his fury at Mr. Cat. Mr. Cat didn't know any English at this time, but the reason for the major's wrath was unmistakable. When he had confronted Nhan and Cuong he had been every bit as angry then as the major was now; but now, as the recipient rather than the bestower of such emotionalism, he was the epitome of coolness. The major shrieked and raged, but Mr. Cat merely smiled and nodded. Later I asked Mr. Cat how he had managed to retain his self-control and not become angry also. He said, "The major was angry already. Why should there be another angry person? Besides, he gained nothing anyway. An angry American major cannot make me change my mind."

With the Dragon's Children

The investigation of Mr. Cat's integrity was still in progress when he had to return to Saigon again for business. As I too had some business to take care of in Saigon, we decided to go together. We were joined by Diep and De, and the four of us took off in the old Chieu Hoi jeep. As we completed our business sooner than anticipated, Mr. Cat suggested that a little vacation was in order because "we have been working too hard." He recommended Vung Tau, a popular beach resort about eighty miles from Saigon.

Shortly thereafter we were bouncing down the rough road toward Vung Tau. Diep drove the jeep and Mr. Cat sat beside him. De (the dogcatcher and soup chef) and I shared the back. It was a beautiful day with the sun shining and patches of greenery dotting the roadside. It was easy to ignore the omnipresent barbed wire and the thick rumbling sounds in the distance.

As we lurched along, Mr. Cat shared his thoughts with us: "The province chief is so hard to get along with. Maybe I should go back to Saigon. I like the people of Go Cong, but it is hard being away from my family." Mr. Cat went on to speak philosophically of war: "War wears on people. It first ruins the body and then takes the soul. It takes everything. There can be no such things as certainty or security."

When we reached Vung Tau, Diep drove us through the streets, along the seashore, and past the outdoor markets. Then we went on to see a famous statue of Buddha on a hill near the town of Vung Tau. The enormous white stone figure dominated the hillside. We inspected the Buddha from all sides, and then removed our shoes to enter the sanctuary of the temple. Mr. Cat approached the altar. Standing, he held three joss sticks with both hands clasped together, bowed his head and, with an up-and-down motion, waved his arms above his head and below his waist three times. Then, deep in meditation, he fell to his knees and went through the same three

- 127 -

David J. Garms

up-and-down movements again. Still on his knees, he leaned forward and placed the joss sticks in an urn by the altar. Then he leaned still farther forward and rested his forehead on the floor of the sanctuary. Finally, he got up, walked over to the contribution box, and placed some money in it.[43]

We continued to drive around Vung Tau town and along the beach. A delicate breeze was blowing, bringing in fresh scents from the South China Sea. Mr. Cat, with his head up and chest out, was fully in command.

"Turn here! Stop! Go straight! Make a right! Change gears!" he ordered Diep.

I couldn't object to Mr. Cat's manner any longer as I had come to recognize that it was necessary for him to display his authority at all times. He was a complex, egotistical, determined little man, but I liked him.

Mr. Cat decided that we should stop at the beach. We took off our shoes and shuffled through the sand awhile, and then we pulled up some chairs under a palm tree. Mr. Cat ordered some beer and steamed clams for all of us. We dug the meat out of the shells with toothpicks and then dipped it in a mixture of salt, pepper, and lime. We loosened up and talked freely with each other. Mr. Cat asked questions about the United States: "Are your elections really fair? Do you also have Communists?"

I tried to answer the questions and then asked a few of my own: "Why do the Vietcong keep fighting? Would the South Vietnamese be willing to accept a Communist government in return for a united Vietnam?"

For several hours we stayed at the beach, relaxing and conversing. Then we started back to Go Cong.

When we returned, we learned that the investigation was in full swing. It was grueling for all of us. National police and personnel from Military Security were frequently visiting the center. The staff and returnees were interviewed several

- 128 -

With the Dragon's Children

times. Chau, Nhan, and Cuong continued their scheming, but though they tried to enlist the support of others, most of the people at the center respected Mr. Cat and refused to say anything against him.

Word of the investigation spread beyond the provincial boundaries. The U.S. senior advisor to the province wrote, requesting from me a full report regarding alleged corruption and extortion of funds in the Go Cong Chieu Hoi Program. Forced out of my neutrality, I wrote a lengthy paper defending Mr. Cat's integrity.

At this point Mr. Cat told me that the province chief was specifically accusing him of selling commodities that had not been authorized for sale. In a sense, this was true. He had sold these commodities to obtain the money to send seventy of our returnees to a Chieu Hoi convention in Can Tho, but he reported that he had done so on the province chief's own specific orders. Funds for such trips had been allocated in the Chieu Hoi budget, but the province chief had refused to authorize their use. Instead, he had ordered the Rural Development chief of Go Cong to issue the commodities to Mr. Cat, and Mr. Cat was then to sell them on the black market and use the money to send the returnees to the convention. The province chief was using this incident to accuse Mr. Cat of illegally selling commodities. If Mr. Cat insisted that he had done so only under orders, the province chief could simply deny it. Even if anyone wanted to take Mr. Cat's side, they would probably withdraw their support under threat of earning the displeasure of the province chief.

The days were long and difficult for Mr. Cat. The Rural Development chief privately advised me, "If you can, please use your influence to encourage Mr. Cat to resign. The outcome cannot be good. The province chief may try to bring him to court."

David J. Garms

Mr. Cat saw what was on the horizon and decided to meet it head-on. He himself requested the case be turned over to the Ministry of Chieu Hoi in Saigon. The province chief balked. He knew that the ministry might well be more sympathetic to Mr. Cat's case. He also realized that Mr. Cat was a far more articulate speaker in public than he. Finally, the province chief conceded that the ministry should review the case, but only if Mr. Cat would leave Go Cong province immediately and forever. Mr. Cat agreed at once. This may, in fact, have been what Mr. Cat had wanted all along. In the case of the province chief, he may have suddenly decided to wash his hands of the matter as it was proving to be more trouble for him than it was worth.

Very shortly thereafter, Mr. Cat left Go Cong. Diep and I drove him into Saigon. I told him that many people in Go Cong understood what he had done, and that from his example they too might find the strength to resist the manipulations of powers greater than themselves.

When we reached Saigon, Mr. Cat and I went to talk with Ogden Williams, chief advisor for the county-wide Chieu Hoi Program. Mr. Williams said that he would speak with the minister of Chieu Hoi about Mr. Cat's case in hopes that the Go Cong experience would not damage Mr. Cat's career in the civil service and, more specifically, that it would not jeopardize his advancement within the ministry.

It soon became apparent that the entire incident had actually improved Mr. Cat's position. He was warmly received by ministry personnel in Saigon and it was obvious that his ability and perseverance had made him something of a hero. Mr. Cat was immediately promoted to a higher position and was decorated by the minister himself with the Psychological Warfare Medal, Second Class. Needless to say, Mr. Cat seemed to be growing more arrogant and authoritarian by the minute—or was it just a facade?

With the Dragon's Children

On the last night in Saigon, Diep and I had dinner with Mr. Cat at the Hotel Continental (Khach-San Continental), a French colonial period hotel. Cat, a committed Francophone, ordered his favorite French red wine, Chateuneuf du Pape. While elegantly sipping from his glass, Cat noted that the Continental Hotel had an important distinction in Saigon. It was among the few businesses foreigners could frequent that had not been attacked by the Vietcong. Cat said that this was because the large open veranda hotel had paid its taxes to the Viet Cong, in addition to the taxes paid to the GVN.

Diep, De and I left Saigon and returned to Go Cong, glad for Mr. Cat but worried for ourselves. Who would be Chieu Hoi chief now? Would the ministry or the province chief win the next skirmish, and how would it affect us?

We didn't have to worry for very long. Trieu again became Chieu Hoi chief of Go Cong. The province chief made the appointment and the ministry quickly approved it. With no difficulty at all, Trieu and I adjusted to working with each other again. Trieu tore into the work just as he had done before. The program lost little momentum because of Mr. Cat's sudden departure. Sometimes it was hard to believe that Trieu had ever left.

CHAPTER VIII

Happy New Year

It was now December, 1967. Trieu decided to temporarily delay construction of a new vocational training building and to give immediate priority to improving the defense perimeter. We were increasingly receiving reports regarding a Vietcong plan to attack the Chieu Hoi Center during Tet. In view of these intelligence reports, Trieu wanted several more bunkers added to the compound. I wondered about his concern since in anticipation of the approaching Tet, the war seemed to have quieted down in many areas of South Vietnam. Trieu said that the situation was unnatural, and that he didn't like it. On the other hand, American counterparts hadn't identified any major threat and were, therefore, advising Vietnamese employees to go home for Tet, 1967. It was clear to me that the Vietnamese had better intelligence than the Americans.

I was eagerly anticipating my first Tet, a combination of the Western Christmas, New Year's, and Easter wrapped into one. Each day my friends in Go Cong told me more about the significance and customs of Tet. It was a time for visiting among friends and relatives. Everyone devoted all they could

With the Dragon's Children

possibly spare of time, effort, and money for repainting their homes, acquiring new clothes, preparing special foods, and making decorations. It was a time to forgive and be forgiven. All negative feelings were to be avoided. The Vietnamese believed that a happy Tet would insure happiness throughout the following year.

With the staff's and returnees' minds focused on Tet, it was difficult for Trieu to complete the improvements of the center's defenses. The war, too, seemed to want to take a holiday, but it was not to happen. Security precautions were let down everywhere in the province. A large proportion of the GVN troops were home visiting their families, and the national police had only a skeletal force in a state of readiness. South Vietnamese everywhere wanted, for a few days, to pretend that there was no war.

On January 30, 1968 all pretenses were shattered when Vietcong and North Vietnamese troops launched a nationwide offensive—something which American and Vietnamese intelligence sources said would not happen. However, Trieu believed that the Vietcong would attack. In most areas, the offensive began without prior warning from either U.S. or GVN intelligence sources. To all of us, it was a paralyzing shock to realize that after years of "losing," the Vietcong were still fully capable of launching a nationwide attack in which the element of surprise was virtually complete.

The failed intelligence leading up to the Tet offensive was widespread. The top CIA officer for Go Cong province, a former Navy SEAL, was a friendly, enthusiastic guy, but he seemed to not be attuned to his environment. He was persistently off the mark with his analyses; his reports regarding the whereabouts of Vietcong were usually out of date.

In my view, the reasons for his faulty analysis were obvious: He did not speak Vietnamese and his interpreter did not have an adequate command of English. In a province where

- 133 -

there were complicated relationships and many nuances, not speaking Vietnamese and having a less than adequate interpreter was dangerous. Also, the CIA officer never did figure out that his interpreter was making fun of him with his Vietnamese friends. Among the Vietnamese, the CIA officer was probably the most talked-about American in the province. He provided entertainment. For example, his vehicle, a green Ford Bronco (all CIA officers in Vietnam were given a green Ford Bronco), was readily recognizable, and when he would drive by the Chieu Hoi Center, the Vietnamese would laugh and shout out, "*Ong Tin Bao. Ong Tin Bao*" (Mr. Intelligence, Mr. Intelligence.) As I traveled about Vietnam, I got the sense that *Ong Tin Bao* was not necessarily unique. If you take the Go Cong situation and multiply it nationwide, this could explain in part why U.S. intelligence was so far off the mark.

As reports of the fighting began to come in, tension replaced shock among the members of the U.S. Advisory Team who served in Go Cong. The province senior advisor briefed us on the situation in the Delta. The capitals of two adjoining provinces had come under heavy attack; Ben Tre in Kien Hoa Province had been overrun, and My Tho in Dinh Tuong Province was partially held by the Vietcong. Where we were standing was twenty miles from Ben Tre and fifteen miles from My Tho.

The U.S senior province advisor requested that all Americans be concentrated in only one compound. As there were no U.S. combat troops present, all members of the team, including civilians, were to set up twenty-four-hour guard duty at the MACV compound. Armed with an M-2 carbine, I stood guard in one section of the compound for the next few nights. It was surprisingly cold those nights. A few miles away, the war was alive with artillery, helicopter gunfire, and bomb drops, but the area immediately surrounding the town was still. My eyes swept the dark areas beyond the compound

With the Dragon's Children

again and again, but each time the shadows were empty. In deafening silence the town waited.

When not on guard duty, I spent all my time at the Chieu Hoi Center. The dread in the eyes of the staff and returnees was sickening to see. We all knew that Chieu Hoi centers throughout the country were being singled out as special targets for attacks. We'd heard that the center in Quang Ngai Province, Region I, had been overrun, and that everyone, staff and returnees alike, had been killed.

Trieu had set up defense plans for the Go Cong Center. His first plan of defense was to try to repel the Vietcong with strikes called in from an ARVN artillery company a few miles away. His second line of defense would be brought into action if the Vietcong broke through the perimeter. In this event, Trieu would call in artillery directly on top of us. Even though the bunkers were soundly constructed, there were bound to be casualties, not only among the Vietcong but among ourselves if this occurred. Trieu requested that all members of the staff move into the bunkers and stay there until the threat of an attack subsided. Whatever their individual thoughts and fears, not one man refused.

Trieu's request and the staff's compliance left me uneasy. I had been excluded because, whatever I might do with the Vietnamese under normal conditions, conditions had now become distinctly abnormal and, as an American, it was thought normal that I face the threat of an imminent attack inside an American compound and in the company of other Americans. Putting aside questions of what was normal and what was not, I asked my immediate supervisor, Lieutenant Colonel (LTC) Yosuru Komoto, for permission to remain in the Chieu Hoi Center.

He hesitated. As a civilian I was supposed to be excluded from situations that might involve combat. I explained, "You know, I've been staying every night at the MACV compound

- 135 -

David J. Garms

with the other Americans, but I think I could be of more assistance if I stayed at the Chieu Hoi Center. Trieu has asked that all staff members remain at the center until the threat is over. I think that my presence might improve their morale. It would show them that the American Advisory Team has confidence in them."

My supervisor agreed, and I moved into the center immediately. I shared one of the bunkers with Trieu. All of us slept on U.S. Army folding cots. The bunker was well supplied. Trieu had a line phone and also a shortwave radio. He had prepared numerous maps of the province and had sketched plans for the defense of the center. There was also a supply of food and water adequate for a short siege. If I had had any hopes left that we would be spared an attack, they evaporated when I saw how Trieu had prepared the bunker.

On February 3, 1968 the day after I moved into the center, the first attack came. The Vietcong stormed the town prison and released 135 political and criminal prisoners. The warden of the prison was killed, and the guards escaped a similar fate only by running away. The province chief's headquarters was right next to the prison. When the attack began, the province chief and some other officials escaped in an armored vehicle to a more secure section of the town. Altogether, there were three U.S. military personnel left on duty that night at the province chief's headquarters. They were able to repel an attack on the headquarters, though one of them was wounded.

When the dawn came, the Vietcong melted back beyond the town limits. The attack on the prison had been successful, and was very well-executed. One Vietcong unit had launched a massive mortar attack on the town to keep the GVN troops inside their bunkers and to divert attention from a ground assault. The Vietcong had been able to enter the town undetected, march right up to the prison doors, and blast the doors

With the Dragon's Children

open before anyone in the town knew that they were among them.

Several more nights passed quietly while we wondered how and where the Vietcong would strike the town next. GVN intelligence reported to Trieu that the Vietcong were planning not just to attack the Chieu Hoi center but to overrun it. They intended to kill the staff members and to capture the returnees. The returnees were to be marched down the road toward the MACV compound where they would be mistaken for Vietcong and shot down by the Americans.

I immediately passed this information to the U.S. Advisory Team. They said that if this happened, "Our first burst of fire will be over their heads. This will give them a chance to disperse. Our next round must be in earnest, though, for how can we be certain whether they are returnees or Vietcong? It is the best that we can do."

Trieu had a better idea. As mentioned earlier, in town there was a Buddhist monk named Minh who had often shown interest in the welfare of the returnees. I had spoken with this monk on a number of occasions, and I was thoroughly impressed with his sensitivity and intelligence. He was a very likeable person and quite a conversationalist. The monk would often come to the center to ask Trieu for permission to address the returnees, and once he even asked to have them visit his pagoda.

Trieu agreed immediately and arranged for the transportation. After the returnees had toured the pagoda, the monk offered them refreshments. He then stood up in the midst of the returnees and began to address them:

"I know that most of you are Buddhist, but if any of you are not, my message will still be relevant.[44] I hope that you will be able to begin a new life now, and the past may be forgotten totally. I believe in peace and love. I long so much for the end of this war that I suffer constant pain. May your prayers also

- 137 -

David J. Garms

ascend to Buddha in the name of peace, and may the power of love and kindness guide us all."

Trieu went to this monk now to ask if the returnees could stay in his pagoda until the threat to their lives was over. The monk was most willing to give refuge to the returnees. By evening all the returnees had been transported from the center to the pagoda. They would be safer there, for the pagoda was in the center of town, and the Vietcong would have had to occupy the entire town in order to harm them. One staff member accompanied them, and he was unarmed. This was a precaution in the event that there were any infiltrators among the returnees. If one or more armed staff members were present, there would have been a temptation for any infiltrators to kill them for the sake of their weapons. A lone, unarmed man presented no temptation at all. There was not too much concern over any infiltrators trying to escape to rejoin their comrades, for this would have meant passing through an entire town that was so on edge that anyone suspicious would be shot at once.

Several more days passed. We waited and the tension grew. By day we could leave the center and move about inside the town, but when night came we took up our positions in the bunkers and waited for the attack.

One morning Trieu said quietly, "I think tonight they will come."

In the afternoon, GVN intelligence informed him that two Vietcong units (later identified as 305th Company and parts of 514th Battalion) of from 100 to 150 men each was grouping in a forested area across the river from the Chieu Hoi Center. Trieu knew that there were two Rural Development (RD) teams stationed in a hamlet near the riverbank. He suspected that the Vietcong would first attack the hamlet from both sides and attempt to annihilate the armed RD teams. The Vietcong knew that an RD team consisted of fifty-nine

With the Dragon's Children

members, and they could therefore expect to outnumber the teams by two or three to one. The two Vietcong units would then join in the assault on the center. The Vietcong might or might not have known how many men would be defending the center itself. In fact, there were only twenty-five of us. Some had had combat experience with the Vietcong or the GVN or both, but others, like me, had no real combat experience.

Trieu had to act fast. He jumped in the jeep and tore down the road and across the river to the hamlet where the RD teams were stationed. He ordered the teams to leave the hamlet in as clandestine a manner as possible and take up positions on the other side of the river near the Chieu Hoi Center. As the river was fairly deep (eight to twelve feet) it served as a natural barrier to a Vietcong advance. However, there was a bridge next to the center, and if the Vietcong crossed it they could make a dash for the center itself. Trieu supervised the quiet repositioning of the RD teams and left them with the words: "No Vietcong will cross the river or the bridge."

It was late afternoon now. Trieu returned to the center and ordered the women clerks to leave for their homes. Then he stationed the rest of us in the bunkers. Trieu and I shared the command bunker. Sergeant Ba was in charge of the rear bunker. Another bunker was shared by Diep and Noi. Cuong manned still another with Thieu, the medic, and Huan, the clerk. Duc-Ba, De and Khai were in other bunkers. Seia was in charge of preparing the weapons and supplying each bunker with ammunition. Bao was out in the field somewhere commanding the APT. Khiet had remained in his district, which I found rather curious.

The night came as we waited in our bunkers. Frightened though we all were, we felt relief to an almost equal degree; whatever would happen during this night, the long waiting was almost over.

- 139 -

David J. Garms

At a few minutes past midnight, the attack began. We could hear the heavy firing of weapons across the river. Trieu let out a shout of glee. His plan had worked! Not realizing that the RD teams had been moved, the two Vietcong units had moved into pincer positions near the hamlet and were firing on each other! The Vietcong were bound to realize their mistake eventually, and they did.[45] The firing died down and then abruptly ceased. The night was silent again.

Agonizing minutes passed as we huddled in our bunkers. Then there was something whistling through the air, and the first mortar hit the center. A mortar platoon of the Vietcong 514th battalion had moved up the river bank and taken up position there to commence firing 82-millimeter mortars into the center. (The U.S. and South Vietnamese forces had 81 millimeter mortars and therefore, the Vietcong could also use this shell in their 82 millimeter mortars, but we couldn't use theirs in ours) A second mortar exploded near us as Trieu frantically grabbed at the phone. He called for artillery support on some pre-established coordinates. Either the coordinates were wrong or the artillery troops were making incorrect calculations, but just after a third mortar hit, we came under a barrage of "friendly" ARVN 105-mm artillery fired directly on our own position.

Trieu snatched at the phone only to discover that the artillery fire had severed the lines. Two more mortars smashed into the center as Trieu got through on the shortwave radio: "Damn it! Not us! Them!"

A second barrage of artillery was fired, but this time it landed far beyond the Vietcong positions. More mortars struck the compound. His face red and his voice cracking, Trieu screamed into the radio: "Damn it! Take your last two coordinates and give us something halfway between them!"

While the ARVN artillery tried to re-determine their coordinates and Vietcong mortars continued to explode in the

- 140 -

With the Dragon's Children

center, my thoughts were not pleasant. What would happen if the Vietcong overran the center and found me, an American? They would hardly be sympathetic toward my status as a non-combatant civilian. I thought of the others in the bunkers too, especially those who had been Vietcong. "No," I thought, "it's better that none of us let ourselves be taken alive."

Then ARVN artillery zeroed in on the Vietcong positions and let loose a barrage so fierce it seemed as though they were trying to make up for their tardiness. The Vietcong attack faltered, then subsided, and finally ceased. Taking nothing for granted, no one slept during the small portion of the night that remained. We continued to scan the perimeter for any Vietcong heads that might appear.

As soon as the sun came up, each of us slowly emerged from his bunker, dazed and blinking. We were all bone-weary and our nerves were in splinters, but no one had been wounded or killed. We began to survey the damage to the center. Noi was relieved to report that everything could be put back right without too much difficulty. As we wandered about the center we heard the roar of a jeep approaching. The jeep came to a sliding halt on the gravel drive of the compound, and the province chief leaped out screaming, *"Trung Uy oi! Trung Uy oi!"* (Oh Lieutenant! Oh Lieutenant!). When Trieu approached, the province chief asked excitedly, "How is everything? Was anyone wounded? What was damaged?"

"I'm happy to report that there were no casualties," Trieu replied. "There was some damage done to the center by friendly artillery, but the damage done by enemy mortars was slight."

The province chief then proposed, "Let's go across the river to see if there are any Vietcong bodies or weapons lying around."

The RD teams joined in searching the area. One body (others were carried off by the Vietcong to prevent American

- 141 -

David J. Garms

and GVN forces from using a body account as an indicator of success), one AK-47 assault weapon, and one Browning .30 caliber machine gun were all that had been left behind.[46] The province chief was so pleased with Trieu that he informed him that the Chieu Hoi Center could keep the machine gun as a reward.

When we returned to the center, Trieu made Sergeant Ba responsible for the machine gun. Ba knew and loved weapons and was excited over his new duty. He gave the weapon a thorough cleaning, after which, without loading it, he cocked it and tested the firing mechanism several times. Ba tried holding the weapon in different positions. Then he bit his lip, faked a mean look, and aimed the weapon at imaginary enemies, shouting, "Bang! Bang! Tat! Tat! Tat! Bang! They're all dead!"

While Ba was playing with the machine gun, Noi went to the pagoda to collect the returnees. Soon he was busy directing them in repairing the damage. There was a great deal of cleaning up to do, but none of the buildings had suffered irreparable damage. Much to everyone's relief, the library/teahouse had been spared significant harm. One goat in the animal husbandry section of the center had been killed by a piece of shrapnel.

Trieu had already directed that the goat be served at a victory breakfast, and De was busy preparing it. He removed the artillery fragments from the carcass, cut it up into small chunks, and then threw it into a pot to which he added red peppers, spices, and vegetables.

Trieu invited me to sit with him in the library/teahouse. We talked about the night's trials and the unexpectedly favorable outcome.

"Ong Gam, you did well last night," Trieu said.

"No," I replied, "you did everything."

With the Dragon's Children

Trieu ordered a case of beer and invited all the staff to join us. De brought in the breakfast of goat meat. Another case of beer was ordered. We began to compliment each other.

"I don't know what would have happened to us without you," Noi said to Trieu.

"I couldn't have done anything without you, Noi," Trieu responded.

As the drinking progressed, the compliments became more and more flattering.

During the weeks following Tet, the number of returnees at the center increased. Many of them were very young peasants who had been recruited by the Vietcong specifically for the Tet offensive. Some had only been Vietcong for a few months. Two of the new returnees had been part of the mortar platoon that attacked the center.

For the next two months, we concentrated on completing the new vocational training building. Construction began as soon as we received some money from the AIK Fund and tin roofing sheets from the Rural Development warehouse. Again, the human element was vital. Everyone at the center was involved in the construction of the new building and could take personal pride in it. When completed, it was a fine structure, even though made entirely out of tin—except for the reinforced cement supporting poles and the wooden rafters.

During the Tet Offensive, I had grown accustomed to sleeping at the center, and even afterward I continued to spend most of my nights there. Besides being the place where I worked, the center had become home to me.

- 143 -

CHAPTER IX

The Professor Who Went to War

In May 1968, Go Cong received a new province chief. It was the policy of Saigon to transfer a chief every two or three years, probably so that he would not come to identify too closely with the people of a particular province. Our province chief was transferred to another province, and Colonel Le Van Tu arrived to replace him.

Colonel Tu was almost the complete opposite of his predecessor. He was tough, but also fair, and his concern for the people of Go Cong was immediately apparent. He not only understood the sense of identity the local people had toward their villages and province, but he actively encouraged it. As a result, there was an upsurge of interest in local government. It was Colonel Tu's avowed belief that the people must first be encouraged to identify with and to participate in local government before any true sense of nationalism could evolve.

One day after his arrival, Colonel Tu came to the Chieu Hoi Center to discuss with me the appointment of a new Chieu Hoi chief. I was surprised that he would take up the matter with me at all, as it was certainly not required of him to

With the Dragon's Children

consult me on any subject. The first I had ever been aware of Mr. Cat's and both of Trieu's appointments was when the men themselves walked into the center and informed me to that effect. I was much impressed with the new province chief's courtesy and sensitivity.

Colonel Tu told me that he wanted to transfer Trieu to the position of RD chief of Go Cong. He greatly admired Trieu's ability and felt that he could be used to even greater advantage as commander of the 3000 RD team members in the province. I was disappointed to lose Trieu again, but I recognized the need for him elsewhere. I also realized that he had succeeded in revitalizing the Chieu Hoi Program in Go Cong to such a degree that it was now possible for it to continue without him.

Colonel Tu told me that he had proposed Lieutenant Pham Thanh Ngoc as Trieu's replacement. Ngoc had been a college professor at the University of My Tho before joining ARVN some ten years before. His specialty was psychological warfare.

Ngoc soon arrived in Go Cong to take up his new post. (The pronunciation of *Ngoc* can be approximated by rhyming it with the English word *mop*.) He had a round, cheerful face with large features. Though he was only in his late thirties, his crew-cut hair was already very gray. His eyes always appeared bloodshot, and he himself liked to attribute this to his vast experience as a dedicated rice wine drinker.

The Chieu Hoi Program in Go Cong had been lucky with Trieu and Mr. Cat and now, incredibly, luck struck a third time. Ngoc possessed almost demoniac enthusiasm and energy. He was continually lecturing the staff and returnees, and he made a point of personally talking with each new returnee. He spoke at all the political education classes and wrote personal letters appealing to the Vietcong to turn themselves in. At the end of the day, Ngoc would still have enough energy to join in the center's recreational activities.

- 145 -

David J. Garms

Ngoc's typical day would start at five in the morning. With none of the moaning and groaning most people go through in the morning, Ngoc would be out of bed and on his feet almost as soon as his eyes were open. The instant his feet touched the floor, Ngoc was on his way to the shower. (The center's single shower consisted of little more than four sheets of tin. The floor was cement, and there was no roof. There was a large earthen water jar in one corner and also a tin can. The bather used the can to scoop water out of the jar and pour the water over himself as he squatted on the cement floor. I used these shower facilities too, and even in the hot season I found the water in the jar so cold early in the morning that it was necessary for me to stifle screams as it trickled down my back.)

By five-thirty, Ngoc would be dressed and at his desk, busy with papers. After his papers were in order he would suggest that we go to breakfast. We usually went to Mr. Uncle's tea shop where breakfast would consist of *pho* (soup with noodles and bits of meat) or *canh* (soup with rice, pig livers, and pig entrails), and *ca phe sua* (strong French coffee mixed with several teaspoons of sweetened condensed milk).

By eight o'clock, we would have returned to the center to find the rest of the staff beginning to arrive. The secretaries would be getting their day's assignments from Khiet, who had recently been promoted to deputy Chieu Hoi chief. Noi would be happily screaming at some returnee for not following an order. The political education course would be starting. Sawing and hammering would be going on in the new vocational training building, and the barber shop would be in operation. Returnees who were not in political indoctrination or vocational training courses would be assigned to some work project such as painting the buildings, sweeping the sidewalks, or preparing food. Ngoc would stroll about the center, observing the various activities, pausing frequently to converse with a staff member or returnee.

- 146 -

With the Dragon's Children

At mid-morning, Ngoc would often suggest that we take a trip to visit a district Chieu Hoi chief or APT members in the field. He would call for an armed guard and we would all pile into the jeep. Ngoc always insisted on driving. We would blast off down the road at the only speed Ngoc recognized—full speed, accomplished by pushing the accelerator all the way to the floor. As the road usually had deep holes and ruts, the jeep would bounce and swerve dangerously all over the road. With Ngoc driving, it never took us more than thirty minutes to reach the farthest point in the province, though those of us who were passengers would have been quite willing to allow more time for the trip.

After reaching our destination, Ngoc and I would spend time talking with whatever persons we had come to see. Lunch was always a problem. Ngoc had very quickly become popular with the people of the province, and everyone wanted him to honor their home. After the decision was made and lunch was eaten, we would sleep for an hour or so on wooden plank beds in one of the homes of the village. We would return to the center by mid-afternoon, and then finish up our work for the day. The staff would usually stop work about six, at which time we would all get ready for volleyball. We played volleyball virtually every day, even at the height of the monsoon season.

These volleyball games were tremendous events, and they lost nothing by daily repetition. The Vietnamese were devoted to this sport, and the people of Go Cong were no exception. Frequently, various teams in the province would play against each other, with the losing team buying a case of beer. On a few separate occasions, some U.S. Advisory Team members had come to play against the Chieu Hoi team, which consisted of both staff and returnees. When it was the Chieu Hoi team against the Americans, I would play with either team. The Americans invariably lost. This gave the Chieu Hoi team enormous pleasure; they would become terribly excited

David J. Garms

over these victories, jumping up and down, laughing, and patting (sometimes pounding) each other on the back.

The volleyball games became particularly amusing when it rained. As the volleyball court was only dirt, after a good rain we would find ourselves playing on thick, slippery mud. We would slip, slide, and fall down all over the court. It was almost impossible to hold on to the ball to serve it, and it was just as difficult to control the ball on a return. Sometimes the server would reach for a fistful of mud from the court and smear it all over the ball just to make things still more difficult. Occasionally the whole situation would get entirely out of control and the volleyball game would degenerate into an outright mud fight. The Vietnamese really loved their volleyball.

Each evening after volleyball, we would shower and then relax a bit over several cups of tea. Later we would have dinner at the center with the returnees, or go out to a small restaurant, or else have dinner at the home of a friend. While we were enjoying our leisurely meal, I found it beyond me to comprehend how such seemingly contented and peaceful people were able to carry on a long, arduous war. I had only to listen for a moment, though, to the dull thud of bombs and shrill bursts of artillery in the distance to know that, somehow, it was indeed possible.

Sometimes, late in the evening, Ngoc would assemble all the returnees together to give them an impromptu lecture on Vietnamese history. It was obvious from these lectures that Ngoc had been a professor in civilian life. His approach was scholarly, even pedantic. The returnees could grasp little of what he said, but they listened intently and were much impressed by the knowledge spread like a feast before them. Ngoc would usually make extensive use of a blackboard during lectures. Often he would draw on it the nations of Asia. He habitually exaggerated the already vast size of China so that it took up virtually the entire blackboard. Vietnam was only

With the Dragon's Children

a tiny speck on the great underbelly of China. Ngoc would then proceed to speak of the history of Vietnam—its ancient culture, its great wars of independence spread over two thousand years, and its inglorious subjugation at the hands of invaders.

At times during these lectures, Ngoc would become very emotional. Tears would start in eyes already so bloodshot that they resembled road maps. Ngoc felt strongly about his country, perhaps too strongly. He was intensely aware of the controversies and conflicts that were tearing his country apart. Often Ngoc would sit at his desk very late at night and by candlelight write out personal appeals to the Vietcong to return. Sometimes he would drink rice wine as he wrote. Sometimes he would weep. Once I asked Diep about Ngoc's weeping, and he said, "Lieutenant Ngoc is a very sensitive human being. He takes all the problems of Vietnam and places them on his shoulders. This is too much of a burden for any man."

Ngoc tried to share his burden to some degree by sharing his extensive knowledge of Vietnamese history. As a foreigner and a friend, I was, to Ngoc's mind, a particularly appropriate target for enlightenment. I had read a good deal on the history of this long-suffering people, but it became even more vivid and far more painful when told by a Vietnamese.

Not long after my arrival in Vietnam I had realized that, for someone to know something of the history of that country, he had only to walk down the streets of any city or town and inquire how the streets had gotten their names. In Saigon the street might be a four-lane boulevard and the name be written on a large, modern sign. In Go Cong the road might be dirt and the name painted crudely on a piece of wood. In still smaller towns the name might not be written anywhere. It didn't matter, though, for the names were always the same. The Vietnamese didn't name their streets after places or things.

David J. Garms

They named them after people—the patriots of Vietnam stretching back across two thousand years.

In Go Cong there was a street called Hai Ba Trung in honor of the Trung sisters. In A.D. 41, after one hundred and fifty years of Chinese rule, the Chinese thought to make their grip still firmer by executing a descendant of the deposed kings of independent Vietnam. His widow and her sister formed an army and personally led it against the Chinese. The Trung sisters succeeded in driving the Chinese from Vietnam, and another independent kingdom was established. It was to last but three years, however, for the Chinese reorganized, returned, and re-conquered. When defeat was certain, the Trung sisters threw themselves in a river and drowned. They were never forgotten by the Vietnamese, and there is virtually not a city or town in Vietnam that does not have a street bearing their name.

The street in Go Cong on which the CORDS compound was located was called Tran Hung Dao after one of Vietnam's greatest generals. In the tenth century, the Vietnamese finally succeeded in winning independence from China, but their independence was severely threatened by their neighbors to the north on many occasions during the following 500 years. The most serious threat rose in the thirteenth century when the Mongol conquerors of China turned their attention southward. They amassed an army of half a million men (coincidentally, the same number of U.S. forces when at its peak) and marched into Vietnam. The Vietnamese general Tran Hung Dao rallied an army of 200,000 to face them. He defeated the Mongols and drove them back into China.

Three years later, Kubla Khan again threw his hordes against Vietnam, and again they were driven back by the army of Tran Hung Dao. In Saigon, Tran Hung Dao Street is, oddly enough, the major boulevard that connects Saigon proper with the predominately Chinese section of Cholon. Also in Saigon,

With the Dragon's Children

an enormous statue of the general overlooks the waterfront. From atop a high pillar he stands in his warrior's garb, his stance stiff and unyielding, with one hand stretched out before him as though he might still defend his people from all who threaten them.

In Go Cong, the street that went by the police station was called Le Loi after the guerrilla who became an emperor. In the fifteenth century the Chinese were finally successful in regaining control over Vietnam. To assist them with administering the subject country, they chose a few indigenous people to become mandarins. Le Loi was one such person. He refused to govern his country in the name of China, however, and instead he raised a guerrilla army of peasants and for ten years waged war against the Chinese. The Chinese were finally driven from Vietnam once more, and Le Loi became the first emperor of the Le Dynasty.

The street in Go Cong that went by the elementary school was called Gia Long. In the seventeenth century, a civil war over succession developed. Independent kingdoms were established in the north and south, and wars between the two raged for a hundred and fifty years. The country was devastated almost beyond salvation. The life, property, and loyalty of the peasants, in both north and south, were pawns in the games of their kings. The heirs to the old dynasty were hunted down and killed even to the remotest descendant.

One escaped, however, and his name was Gia Long. He survived a fugitive childhood, and as a young man went to the western provinces to raise an army. He began a war of unification, one of the bloodiest in the history of a people who had known so much of bloody wars. Finally, in 1802, Vietnam was united once again. Gia Long proclaimed himself emperor of a new dynasty, the Nguyen. It was to be the last of Vietnam's many dynasties.

David J. Garms

By the military hospital on the outskirts of Go Cong was a street named Phan Thanh Gian, after an early martyr of French colonialism. The French had begun to arrive at a most inopportune time in the history of the Asian nation. Early in the nineteenth century, when French traders and missionaries (and the soldiers to protect them) had become a force which the Vietnamese could no longer ignore, the country was still struggling to recover from the effects of its recent great civil war. The French were gradually swallowing the kingdom province by province. The emperor had had to concede to the French the control of the southern provinces (including Saigon), but still held hopes of retaining authority over the central and northern provinces.

His hopes dwindled with the shelling by French warships of the harbor of Da Nang in Central Vietnam. The emperor sent Phan Thanh Gian, a respected scholar and his most trusted diplomat, to negotiate with the French in Paris for the most favorable deal possible. Phan Thanh Gian was a clever negotiator (and when have the Vietnamese not been so?), and he managed to extract the promise that France would limit herself to control of external trade and foreign relations. He had left Paris and was en route home when he learned that the French were marching inland from the coast. Phan Thanh Gian returned to Saigon, locked himself in his home, and fasted until he died. His last words were to demand of his sons the promise that they would never collaborate with the French.

A street in Go Cong on which there were many small shops was named Phan Ding Phung after a scholar who turned revolutionary. France never knew peace in her new colony; revolts, some of major consequence, took place almost without respite. The most serious revolt in the last part of the nineteenth century was led by a retiring scholar, Dr. Phan Ding Phung. He and three thousand followers began a revolt

- 152 -

With the Dragon's Children

which took the French ten years to put down. The guerrilla tactics learned and practiced under his leadership were developed and refined by the Vietnamese before the names of Mao Tse Tung and Ho Chi Minh were known. Phan Ding Phung himself died of illness and hardship at his mountain retreat in 1895. The remnants of his followers surrendered on a promise of pardon, though beheading rather than pardon was what awaited them.

These were the names of some of the streets in Go Cong. The same names had been given streets in Saigon, Can Tho, Hue, Da Nang, Nha Trang, Vung Tau, and towns so insignificant that their names were not known outside the country. These names were part of the heritage of all Vietnamese, and so I was not surprised to be told that the same names could be found in cities and towns in North Vietnam.

I found myself wondering what twentieth-century names would be added to the roster of patriots. Surely there would be a few names, even though Vietnamese history was so cluttered with wars, heroes, and martyrs. I became convinced that, if I were to walk the cities, towns, and hamlets of both Vietnams and to ask each person I met, "Who is a modern patriot?"—assuming I was given honest answers—then this century would already have produced one such person. That person would be Ho Chi Minh.

The majority of the people might be unable to comprehend the man's political orientations, and some of those who could might not be convinced, but I could not escape the impression that whatever the Vietnamese thought of the man's orientations, they revered the man himself. Whatever else Ho Chi Minh had accomplished or tried to accomplish, he had led his people to victory over the French. Knowing how even the South Vietnamese regarded him, it was not surprising to see streets called Ho Chi Minh and even a city (Saigon)

- 153 -

David J. Garms

named after him only two years after the first edition of this book was published in 1973.

Ngoc might weep when he compared Vietnam's past with its present, but he could also be a very tough individual. On several occasions I saw him knock an APT member to his knees when he had gotten out of line. He explained to me that these were hardened, often brutal men who could best be "reasoned with" physically. (I often wondered how violence could eventually lead to non-violence.)

Ngoc always had a reason for resorting to violence. On one occasion, an APT member had seduced a village girl. As soon as the offense was known, the police seized the man and threw him into the provincial jail. When he learned of this, Ngoc stormed into the jail, demanding to see the prisoner. Once he was standing before the cell, Ngoc demanded that the cell be opened so that he could question the prisoner personally. The police chief was standing by and he agreed to this. Ngoc then began to question the APT member about the trouble with the village girl. Seemingly unsatisfied with the response the prisoner made, Ngoc suddenly became horribly violent. He began to beat the man severely. The APT member fell to his knees, tried to cover his bleeding face, and screamed for mercy. Ngoc continued with the beating until the police chief, unable to bear any more, shouted, "Stop! He has received his punishment! I order this man released at once!"

Immediately Ngoc stopped, and shortly thereafter he returned to the center with the APT member. As Ngoc enjoyed explaining later, the whole display of violence had been for the viewing benefit of the police chief. Ngoc actually liked this APT member and he knew that, unless something unorthodox was attempted, the man could easily remain in jail for months. Hence, Ngoc had taken it upon himself to punish the offender, and in so visible and brutal a manner that the police chief was moved to order his immediate release. The APT member, after

With the Dragon's Children

he had recovered somewhat from his beating, realized this, and he became an even more devoted friend and subordinate of Ngoc.

In July 1968, a dream of many people at the Chieu Hoi Center came true; Go Cong was officially recognized as having one of the finest Chieu Hoi Programs in the nation. During several four-week periods of the first seven months of 1968, Go Cong led all the other provinces in the number of new returnees received. A lot of people had brought this about. There was Trieu, of course, who had twice taken up the burden of leading the program. I thought of Mr. Cat off in Saigon struggling with paperwork; he would have heard the news, and I knew how pleased he would be to know that the promise he had made at the dedication of the library/teahouse had been kept. Ngoc had joined the center later, but he had picked up where the others left off, and the program had continued to move forward. Most of all, I thought of men like Noi, Diep, Duc-Ba, Khiet, and Sergeant Ba—the men who had always been there and who had always done their job, regardless of the circumstances.

For some time, Odgen Williams, chief advisor of the Chieu Hoi Program, had been suggesting that I leave Go Cong as "the program there is on the way and help is desperately needed in Hue." (During the Tet Offensive, the Chieu Hoi chief of Hue had been killed and the center completely destroyed. Several months afterward, the program there was still in shambles.) Ngoc was very upset when he learned of my transfer. He wrote a personal letter to Mr. Williams requesting that I be allowed to remain in Go Cong.

The wheels were already in motion, though, and now I myself did not wish that they should be halted. In August I agreed to go to Hue. Perhaps my feeling was something like that of Trieu's when he accepted the position of RD chief. Like him, I had been happy at the Go Cong Chieu Hoi Center, but I too could not pretend that there was no other work to be done.

- 155 -

David J. Garms

The center could get along without me now (as, indeed, might always have been the case). Whatever contributions I might have been able to make, I had already either made them or forever lost the chance. Hue offered new experiences and new challenges, and I found myself unable to resist recognizing that it was time to move on.

Once Ngoc was able to accept that I would be leaving, he began to lecture me on what I would find in Hue:

"Hue is the ancient capital of Vietnam. You will become enchanted by its beauty and wrapped up in its history. You will enjoy walking along the Perfume River, and visiting the Citadel, the Imperial Palace, and the tombs of the emperors. I fear, though, that you will not see happiness there. The people cannot forget that for so long they were the center of culture, religion, and government. They are Central Vietnamese, and they do not like the South or North Vietnamese. The land is not so rich in Central Vietnam, and the people are poorer. They try to ignore their loss of power and their poverty by putting on a facade of cultural and intellectual sophistication and by practicing political intrigue. The war has been harder there, too. Because of their own inclinations, and because of their proximity to the Demilitarized Zone, the people have given more support to the Vietcong and the North Vietnamese. This has caused heavy retaliation from GVN and American forces. Finally, I must warn you to be careful. It is said that a man can die more easily in Hue than anywhere else. It is a bitter, unhappy place."

I tried to make as little as possible of my departure, but Ngoc insisted upon giving a farewell party for me the night before I was to leave. It was rather much like many of the parties we had had before, and from all outward appearances it was not a sorrowful occasion. Ngoc formally presented me with two captured prizes—a Russian-made K-45 bolt-action rifle, and a Vietcong flag. I slept at the Chieu Hoi Center my

- 156 -

With the Dragon's Children

last night, but then I'd been staying there nights for many months anyway.

Early the next morning, I got into the Chieu Hoi jeep with Diep, who had insisted upon driving me into Saigon. Some of my friends had also got up early, and they gathered around the jeep. Diep started up the engine, and the jeep began to move down the road.

"*Tra lai! Tra lai!*" (Come back! Come back!) I heard someone calling.

"*Toi se tra lai! Toi se tra lai!*" (I will! I will!) I called back.

CHAPTER X

Aftermath

It is surprising how fast South Vietnam fell after the conventional North Vietnamese Army divisions crossed the DMZ in 1975. The president of Vietnam, Nguyen Van Thieu fled the country and traveled to Taiwan. The vice president, Nguyen Cao Ky, fled for the U.S. He opened a liquor store in Los Angeles. General Minh assumed the presidency. Minh saw the hand writing on the wall and ordered that all South Vietnamese units surrender to the North Vietnamese and Vietcong forces. Most did but some didn't. For example, there was a rearguard action in Long An province, which is just south of Saigon. Reportedly, Colonel Tu (the former province chief of Go Cong) was in charge of this action. Trieu went to join him and was, reportedly, killed in action.

There were many reports that there would be a blood bath when the North Vietnamese took over. Fortunately, this did not happen. However, all those who worked for the South

With the Dragon's Children

Vietnamese government were required to take political indoctrination courses.

A question remains as to whether any of my colleagues at the Chieu Hoi center were double agents. For example, I found Khiet's absence during the Tet offensive to be curious, particularly now that he had been promoted to Deputy Chieu Hoi chief for the province. Was he possibly a double agent?

Appendix I

Chieu Hoi Education Guidelines

I. Outline Summary of Standard Procedures for Political Education of Hoi Chanh

Objectives of Political Education: A) To give the returnees a chance to know the errors of communism and the facts of life in South Vietnam in order to help them develop a strong anti-Communist attitude; and B) To present fundamental democratic procedures that will permit returnees to adapt themselves easily to the national community.

II. Principles of Political Education:

A. Education materials are intended only as guides;

B. Returnees will be free to express their views;

C. Political education courses are to be held in the form of lectures and discussions rather than as school classes; and

D. Returnees are to be given a basic knowledge of national life so as to be able to develop anti-Communist beliefs.

With the Dragon's Children

III. Educational Psychology and Techniques:

A. Avoid too much leisure time;

B. Create conditions that will permit returnees to enjoy a life sufficiently comfortable to ease anxiety during the early days of their return;

C. Give returnees the opportunity to visit with their families and relatives;

D. Expedite necessary paperwork and formalities before proceeding with political education; and

E. Class size requirements and duration.

　　1. All returnees will receive political indoctrination during their required two-month stay at the center, and no returnee can leave the center to resume a normal life until completing the course. In extreme cases, the status of the returnee could be changed to that of a prisoner of war;

　　2. Duration of the classes will be sixty days for the provincial and city centers, no less than forty days for regional centers, and up to sixty days for the national center;

　　3. The number of returnees for each course must be no less than twenty and no more than one hundred and fifty; and

　　4. Repeat courses will be permitted only under such circumstances as illness or at the request of a returnee with a valid reason.

IV. Teaching Emphases, Required

David J. Garms

Subjects, and Time Per Subject

A. Required subjects and recommended durations:

1. Chieu Hoi policy (eight hours); and

2. Understanding and evaluating Communist systems:

   a. Political regimes and economic systems in the world (four hours);

   b. Errors in the Communist economic system in practice (four hours);

   c. Realistic look at communism in Vietnam, including terrorism and propaganda (four hours);

   d. The split in the Russian-Chinese block, revisionism, and dogmatism (four hours);

   e. Communist agricultural policy in North Vietnam (four hours);

   f. Communism and religion (two hours); and

   g. Truth about Communist leaders —(Mao Tse Tung, Ho Chi Minh, Vo Nguyen Giap)— (two hours).

3. History of Vietnam's struggles:

   a. Struggles of Vietnamese people against Chinese invaders, the French, and the Communists (eight hours);

   b. Comparison of forces of freedom and communism (four hours);

With the Dragon's Children

    c. Present economic, political, and social conditions in the Republic of Vietnam and the certainty of victory (four hours);

    d. Necessary presence of Allied Forces in South Vietnam (four hours); and

    e. The Free World's aid to the Republic of Vietnam in comparison with Russian and Chinese aid to North Vietnam (four hours).

4. Law:

    a. Republic of Vietnam's constitution (four hours); and

    b. Citizen's rights and duties (four hours).

5. Conclusion:

    a. Attitude of the Hoi Chanh toward his country (one hour); and

    b. Attitude of the Hoi Chanh toward his fellow citizens (one hour).

B. Time emphasis for each course:

1. Lectures will account for 50 percent of the total time;

2. Group discussions will take up 25 percent of the time; and

3. Question and answer sessions will take up the remaining 25 percent.

V. Instructors:

A. Selection of instructors is limited to those who are qualified to teach the subjects and who are effective persuaders and staunch anti-Communists;

B. Specialists from Allied agencies will be invited to teach only technical subjects, and they will not lecture to the returnees on politics;

C. Those centers which had no qualified instructors may request the ministry to assign instructors to them for temporary duty; and

D. The ministry will hold seminars to train staff or APT members who would make competent instructors with additional training.

VI. Instruction Materials:

A. Only those topics and materials which have been approved and issued by the ministry will be used:

1. Other topics and materials may be added only if they are compatible with the political education guidelines as prescribed; and

2. Additional materials may be used only if the use of them is mentioned in official reports to the ministry.

B. Current events should be emphasized to the maximum in order to deter enemy propaganda concerning daily developments; and

C. Centers should make the best possible use of audio-visual techniques and other educational aids.

With the Dragon's Children

VII. *Class Organization:*

A. A manager will have overall responsibility for political indoctrination:

1. As he represents not only the Chieu Hoi Program, but all anti-Communist nationalists, his influence and prestige are important;

2. He is to work for the affection and esteem of the returnees and should be regarded by them as an indulgent brother;

3. He will correctly implement all instructions from the ministry regarding political education; and

4. He will periodically review the work of the teaching staff.

A. A supervisor will provide for living quarters and security and will keep track of the whereabouts of all returnees;

B. A director of courses will be appointed to map out programs of activity, be concerned with the morale of the returnees, and encourage returnees' aspirations; and

C. Instructors, under the supervision of the manager and director of courses, will teach the political education courses.

VIII. *Self-organization, Discipline, and Incentives:*

A. All returnees living in centers are to be regarded as elements of a community;

B. Due to the requirements of security and in order to induce the spirit of model citizens of the Republic

- 165 -

of Vietnam, discipline will be regarded as a priority concern; and.

C. Returnees shall be in organizational divisions as follows:

   1. Cell – from two to five persons;

   2. Team – from two to five cells;

   3. Inter-team – from two to three teams; and

   4. Group – several inter-teams in the same training course.

D. Returnees in all groups will vote for cell leaders, team leaders, inter-team leaders, and group leaders, but maximum cooperation among all groups shall be promoted:

   1. Special attention should be given to elections in order to give the returnees first-hand experience with democratic processes; and

   2. Committees may be formed to assist with publications, recreation, maintenance, and food preparation.

E. All centers must display their regulations, and all regulations should meticulously define matters relating to both individual and collective activities of the returnees during their stay at the center; and

F. In the matter of discipline, as returnees should be encouraged to come to conclusions by their own thought processes, those who fail to do so must be re-educated in order to recognize their faults by any of the following techniques:

With the Dragon's Children

1. Discussion;

2. Self-evaluation;

3. Public warning;

4. Deprivation of allowances and privileges;

5. Loss of rights to attend vocational training courses; and

6. Loss of military deferment privileges upon release.

G. If, after the political education course is complete, there are indications that a returnee remains confused and is still pro-Communist, the center will turn him over to the national police and the decision will be made to:

1. Have him undergo further indoctrination; and

2. Be subjected to disciplinary measures.

H. To make political education fruitful, it is necessary to make use of such incentives and rewards as:

1. The election of the outstanding returnee of the week;

2. Commendation letters from the manager of the center;

3. Priority in realizing aspirations, particularly admission to the APT.

David J. Garms

IX. Course Implementation:

A. Formal opening and closing ceremonies for each political education course are necessary to make the experience memorable:

  1. A definite program for the ceremonies should be followed; and

  2. Speeches, responses, and expressions of thanks should be sincere.

B. The following ways of increasing motivation are suggested:

  1. Give clearer explanations to those who do not understand;

  2. Favor those who work hard;

  3. Organize awards and ceremonies; and

  4. Entertain returnees with recreation, movies, parties, and by reading them literary works.

C. Instructors' attitudes and duties:

  1. Instructors should produce facts and avoid one-sided arguments to defend a matter; proof should be used to help the listeners' reason correctly according to the purpose of the presentation:

  2. As political subjects are aired, too much theory should be avoided;

  3. Documents printed by the ministry should be used as guides and not be read to the returnees directly;

- 168 -

With the Dragon's Children

4. Use of Communist-invented words, particularly the harmful ones which portray us in a passive position must not be used; the Communists in North Vietnam and the Communists in South Vietnam are to be called by the compulsory names "North Vietcong" and "South Vietcong," and use of "Front for the Liberation of South Vietnam" is strictly forbidden to indicate the latter;

5. Instructors should encourage the returnees to express their intimate thoughts and feelings;

6. Discussions should be terminated when everyone had expressed an opinion, and all opinions expressed are found to conform to those of the majority;

7. When a reply must be made to questions concerning corrupt practices in our society, the instructors should point out that these practices are only temporary and will be terminated sooner or later; and

8. Particular attention must be given to those returnees who have spent many years with the enemy:

   a. Their errors must be carefully explained;

   b. Instructors must be clever and subtle in their explanations to help such returnees make more accurate judgments; and

   c. The instructors must create confidence among these returnees that we will decisively defeat the Communists.

- 169 -

David J. Garms

9. If, during formal class hours, a returnee has not expressed his opinions, he should be encouraged to do so in his cell, team, inter-team, or group; regardless of where he does it, the returnee should be subtly persuaded to express his opinions.

X. Indirect Forms of Political Training:

A. The following specific points regarding informal forms of instruction should be considered:

1. Each member of the staff must be prepared to chat with the returnees whenever opportunities are available and, most of all, to talk in small groups while eating, playing, or resting;

2. During formal and informal talks, staff members should attempt to add some anti-Communist sidelights on even apparently apolitical topics; and

3. Although there is no specified program for this, each member of the staff should try to talk with each returnee at least once a week.

B. Opportunities for returnees to visit military and civilian installations and facilities should not be missed as they carve into the memory pictures which provoke reflection.

C. It is recommended that libraries be set up to enable returnees to read politically sound magazines and novels and scientific and historical books.

XI. Allocation, Authorization, and

With the Dragon's Children

Utilization of Political Training Funds:

A. Under the Chieu Hoi budget for 1968, the working figure of 500 piasters has been allocated for each returnee for the specific purpose of political education.

B. The suggested breakdown for expenditures is as follows:

1. Materials for writing and reproduction of training and test materials (70 piasters);

2. Photographs for returnee to keep or send to family (160 piasters);

3. Prizes for outstanding graduates (80 piasters);

4. Weekly incentive prizes (10 piasters);

5. Dinner party marking the graduation ceremony (100 piasters);

6. Materials for making charts and tables, photos, slides, and batteries for loudspeakers and tape recorders (30 piasters);

7. Decorations for opening and closing ceremonies, including banners and flowers (20 piasters);

8. Wall posters and publications dealing with course activities (10 piasters);

9. Sundry and unforeseen requirements of the course, such as refreshments for the instructors and the procurement of sport and recreational equipment (20 piasters).

XII. Authorization to Begin Political

David J. Garms

Education Courses:

A. Province centers must request authorization from the province chief before beginning a course and

B. National, regional, and city centers must request authorization from the ministry before beginning a course.

Appendix II

Endnotes

1. The forty-four provinces of South Vietnam were divided into four regions or corps. Stretching south from the Demilitarized Zone they were Region I (or I Corps) with its capital at Da Nang; Region II (or II Corps) with its capital at Nha Trang; Region III (III Corps) with its capital at Bien Hoa (near Saigon); and Region IV (IV Corps) with its capital at Can Tho.

2. U.S. Army Colonel Charles T.R. Bohannan was the primary U.S. advisor to the Philippine government during the Huk Bal Huk insurgency (1946 – 1954) and Sir Robert Thompson was the primary British government advisor with the Malaysia counterinsurgency program (1963 – 1966). Both Colonel Bohannan and Sir Robert Thompson advised the GVN regarding the establishment of a nationwide Chieu Hoi (Returnee) program. Sir Robert was also, at the same time, an advisor to President Ngo Dinh Diem and to both Presidents Kennedy and Nixon. Additional information may be

- 173 -

found in the following: http://en.wikipedia.org/wiki/
Robert_Grainger_Ker_Thompson.

3.   Australians had been assigned to the Chieu Hoi Program
     as part of their government's assistance to the war effort.
     Filipinos were hired through a Manila-based company
     called the Eastern Construction Company, Inc. They were
     assigned to the program partially because it was thought
     that their experience with the Huks would be relevant to
     Vietnam, and partially because they could be hired and
     placed in assignments more quickly. In an attempt to
     diversify the staff, and to achieve an American presence
     at all levels, a few Americans were assigned to the Chieu
     Hoi program beginning in 1967.

4.   The Swiss-made Pilatus Porter jet-prop aircraft had
     excellent short take-off and landing (STOL) capabilities.
     The Swiss often used the aircraft to pick-up skiers
     who had gotten marooned in the Alps. In Vietnam, the
     aircraft was an excellent choice for the small airstrips in
     provincial capitals.

5.   There were a total of fifty-two Chieu Hoi centers in
     Vietnam: a national center in Saigon, a regional center
     in each of the four regions, a provincial center in each
     of the forty-four provinces, and separate city centers in
     Vung Tau, Cam Ranh, and Da Nang. Centers varied
     considerably in size, depending on the proven and
     anticipated returnee rate. Provincial and city centers
     had a capacity of between 100 and 200 returnees, and
     as indoctrination lasted two months, a six-times-a-year
     turnover was expected. Regional centers, also with a
     turnover every two months, could accommodate about
     400 at a time. The national center in Saigon, with a
     turnover four times a year, was being expanded to achieve

With the Dragon's Children

a capacity of 1000. If all fifty-two centers were filled to capacity at all times, it would be possible to accommodate a nationwide total of more than 60,000 returnees a year.

6. Two kinds of beer are produced in Vietnam. The smaller bottle is called Biere Ba Buoi Ba (Thirty-three Beer) or Biere Nho (Small Beer). The larger bottle is called Biere Larue, the original trademark of the French-founded "Brasseries et Glacieres d'Indochine." The company is still partially French-owned and managed. A colloquial name for the larger beer is Biere Con Cop (Tiger Beer), partially derived from a tiger's face on the bottle, and partially because the Vietnamese like to say, "If you drink too much Biere Con Cop, you will turn into a screaming tiger."

7. As Vietnamese have great difficulty pronouncing final r's and s's, Gam was the closest they could get to Garms. They continued to address me by my last name, because, in their own culture, the given name follows rather than precedes the family name, and it is the given rather than the family name that is used even between persons who are not close friends. For example, in the case of Le Ngoc Diep, Le is the family name, Ngoc is the middle name, and Diep is the given name. He was called Ong Diep (Mr. Diep) by the general public and simply "Diep" by his close friends. The family name is not used at all except for official and ceremonial purposes.

8. Go Cong means peacock hill, a rather misleading choice of names as the province has very few hills and no peacocks at all.

9. These statistics are based on estimates made by CORDS and Vietnamese province officials.

David J. Garms

10. Details regarding MACV may be found in the following document: http://en.wikipedia.org/wiki/ Military_Assistance_Command,_Vietnam.

11. To discover leaders on the non-national level who are elected rather than appointed, one has to go all the way down to the hamlet level. Despite noises made by both the GVN and the United States governments about "bringing democracy to Vietnam," the Vietnamese people, in fact, have long enjoyed democracy (though without giving it that name) at this particular level. They lost this privilege only under the regime of President Diem, who apparently feared such elections would permit Communists to win office.

12. Grinter, Lawrence E. Amnesty in South Vietnam: An Analysis of the Chieu Hoi Program. Simulmatics Corp. funded by the Department of Defense, Washington, DC, 1967.

13. At the 1967 official rate of exchange of 118 piasters to $1, this was the equivalent of about $84. In 1970 the official rate of exchange was changed to 275 piasters to $1, and at this much more realistic figure, Trieu's salary would be about equal to $36.

14. The breakdown for Go Cong was as follows: 65 percent had been small farmers before joining the Vietcong; 20 percent had been laborers; and 10 percent had been involved with trade. This left five percent who had comprised something of an intelligentsia.

15. Prominent among such exceptions were members of the NVA (North Vietnamese Army). They were tenacious fighters and, as a rule, were deeply committed politically. They comprised only a small minority of returnees

- 176 -

With the Dragon's Children

nationwide because their numbers were fewer in proportion to the South Vietnamese Vietcong, because they were far less likely to change their minds about the conflict, and because one of the most effective appeals to a would-be returnee—that he would be able to return to his home and family—could not apply to them. NVA returnees are given little attention in this book because, during the time I was in Go Cong, there were only a handful of them in the entire Delta, and none at all in Go Cong.

16. _____The Chieu Hoi Program: Questions and Answers, Chieu Hoi Directorate, MACCORDS, Saigon, 1970.

17. In addition to food, clothing, and shelter, a returnee received a monthly allowance of 300 piasters (about $2.50 at the 1967 rate of exchange) while he/she was in the center.

18. Ha had had many close friends among the Vietcong, and he never forgot them, even after returning to the GVN, as I realized one day when Ha and I were driving by the scene of a recent skirmish. He asked me to stop the jeep so that he could inspect a Vietcong body lying near the roadside. He returned to the jeep shortly thereafter, and we drove on several more miles before Ha spoke again. When he did, it was simply to say, "He was my friend."

19. In Chieu Hoi Centers in some of the other provinces, it was a policy to dress the returnees in distinctive clothing.

20. In the May 1, 1971 issue of "Pacific Stars and Stripes," a former OSS agent named Lawrence Vogt revealed how he and five other Americans spent three months behind Japanese lines in what is now North Vietnam, helping to

- 177 -

David J. Garms

train about a hundred Vietnamese guerrillas. Vogt stated that Ho Chi Minh and Vo Nguyen Giap were with them most of the time, and that he still has a picture taken of himself with Giap, the late defense minister of North Vietnam and the architect of the French defeat at Dien Bien Phu.

21. Circular #211, Ministry of Chieu Hoi, Saigon, 1970.

22. For a period of time there was one additional motivation. In December, 1968, the ministry put into effect the Third Party Inducement Policy. Under this program a person who induced a Vietcong to return would receive a cash award. The award varied from the equivalent of $35 for the return of a local force member to $2,800 for the return of the military commander of an entire region. The program was abandoned about six months after it went into effect, partially due to the fact that it appeared that a number of clever citizens were turning each other in for the sake of the award, and the "inducer" and the "Vietcong" were splitting the money between them. I have not discussed this policy further as it did not take effect until after I had left Go Cong.

23. Grinter, Lawrence E., Amnesty in South Vietnam: An Analysis of the Chieu Hoi Program.

24. In 1969, the period of automatic deferment was reduced to six months.

25. As there were no U.S. combat units stationed in Go Cong, there were also no Kit Carson Scouts present.

26. Most returnees in Go Cong did not return to the Vietcong by either force or choice, but Manh's case, though not typical, was also not unique.

With the Dragon's Children

27. A natural reaction to a case such as Duc's—a mere boy who had not become a Vietcong willingly and who had deserted when the opportunity arose—would be to dispense with the mandatory stay at the center and send him home to his mother. For several reasons, however, the Go Cong Chieu Hoi staff was wise to comply with regulations; to send him home would be to expose him to the danger of being killed or conscripted again, and to keep him at the center might prove valuable for the vocational training it offered him.

28. Le Thanh Khoi, Le Viet-Nam: Histoire et civilisation, Paris, 1955, p. 204, quoted in The Smaller Dragon, by Joseph Buttinger, Frederick A. Praeger, New York, 1958, p. 154.

29. A political commissar was in charge of overall indoctrination of a Vietcong unit. He had the authority to decide if the unit was psychologically prepared to go into battle or if it needed further political training.

30. Bao barely accepted the authority of the province chef.

31. Bao did not go through the political re-education program at the Chieu Hoi center in Go Cong. Returning Vietcong who held important positions were sent to Saigon for education and training.

32. Nuoc mam (fish sauce) is made of fermented fish that is heavily salted, ground up, and then strained. It has an extremely strong odor. The Vietnamese use it to season almost every dish.

33. During one trip to Minnesota, I told my brother, Dan, about the South-East Asians fondness for dog meat. The town in which my brother lived had some recent arrivals

- 179 -

David J. Garms

from Cambodia and Vietnam. After I alerted my brother regarding the dog-eating tradition, he said he started paying more attention to any "missing dog" problems in the town. Sure enough, periodically a dog "went missing." As my brother didn't want to lose his dog, he decided to be proactive; he advised the Vietnamese and Cambodians that his lips were sealed as long as they left his dog alone. The reply he received was "No problem, your dog too little."

34. The Vietcong's official policy limited recruitment from age sixteen to age thirty-seven. In practice, however, it was not strictly enforced.

35. As polygamy was illegal, the "small wife" and her children had no legal status. However, most men made private provisions for the security of their second families. Further, even young, attractive, and comparatively well-educated Vietnamese women were not always loathe to become a "small wife." With so many eligible men either dead or away at war, they were simply being realistic about their situation.

36. In Vietnam, women retain their maiden name after marriage. They take their husband's name ordinarily only when the husband and wife are referred to as a unit. For example, Mrs. Huong would become Mrs. Chi when someone wished to speak of "Mr. and Mrs. Chi."

37. Like Bao, Khiet had received his re-indoctrination at the national center in Saigon.

38. An unofficial estimate in "The Evening Star," Washington, D. C., December 9, 1968 was $40,000.

With the Dragon's Children

39. There were other lives spared as well: American and Vietnamese lives that might have been lost in bringing about a Vietcong's death.

40. This Spanish medical team was the Government of Spain's total contribution to the war effort.

41. Throughout his tirade, Mr. Cat addressed Nhan and Cuong as *mai*. This is a very disrespectful form of you and is seldom used. *Ong* is the polite masculine you. *Ba* is the equivalent for married women and *co* for unmarried women. *Anh* is used for older brothers, but can also be used to refer to close male friends. *Chi* is used for older sisters or close female friends. *Em* refers to younger brothers and sisters. Husband and wife may refer to each other as *anh* and *em*.

42. His actions followed traditional Buddhist practice in Vietnam.

43. In fact, of the one thousand returnees I worked with in Go Cong, I never knew of one who was not Buddhist by heritage if not in practice.

44. Rural Development teams were assigned to each province. A fifty-nine-member team would enter a contested village and live there for a period of time for the purpose of developing the village economically, identifying local VC, and instilling in the inhabitants some sense of identification with the GVN.

45. Vietcong units were often armed partially with captured weapons and therefore could not necessarily distinguish the sounds of enemy fire from the fire of their own units. For example, the Vietcong's 82 mm mortar may not be distinguishable from the American's 81 mm mortar,

- 181 -

particularly when the Vietcong were using captured 81 mm shells in their 82 mm mortar tubes. The sound of the American M-16 and Vietcong AK-47 are substantially different. As far as the Vietcong body count goes, the Vietcong made every effort to remove all bodies from the battlefield as they knew that Americans were using the number of bodies counted on the battlefield as an indicator of success.

46. Circular 495, Ministry of Chieu Hoi, Saigon, 1968. The document is extremely interesting, but it is also more than forty pages long and often repetitious. I have condensed and simplified it, but though I have altered its form considerably, I have not changed the content or the spirit of the document to any significant degree. Except for the change in length and form, it is as exact a reproduction as I could make it.

Appendix III

Selected Bibliography

1. Appy, Christian G., Patriots, New York: Penguin Books, 2003

2. Behnke, James, Dai-Uy, Bisbee, AZ: Taylor Desktop Publishing, 1992.

3. Brochex, Pierce, Ho Chi Minh - A Biography, Cambridge, UK: Cambridge University Press, 1975.

4. Buttinger, Joseph, The Smaller Dragon, New York, NY: Frederick A. Praeger,1958

5. Dellinger, David, Vietnam Revisited: From Covert Action to Invasion to Reconstruction, Boston: South End Press, 1986.

6. Ellsberg, Daniel. A Memoir of Vietnam and the Pentagon Papers, New York, NY: Penguin Books, 2002.

7. Ellsberg, Daniel, Papers on the War, New York, NY: Simon and Schuster, 1972.

David J. Garms

8. Fall, Bernard. Last Reflections on a War. Garden City, NY: Doubleday, 1967.

9. Grinter, Lawrence E. Amnesty in South Vietnam: An Analysis of the Chieu Hoi Program. Chapel Hill, NC: Simulmatics Corp. Funded by the Department of Defense, 1967.

10. Karnow, Stanley. Vietnam: A History. New York, NY: Penguin Books, 1983.

11. Koch, J.A., The Chieu Hoi Program in Vietnam, 1963 – 1971, Advanced Research Projects Agency, Department of Defense, Washington, D.C. by Rand Corp., declassified 2005.

12. Lomperis, Timothy J., Reading the Wind: The Literature of the Vietnam War, Durham, NC: Duke University Press, 1987.

13. Marr, David. Vietnamese Anticolonialism, 1885 – 1925, Berkeley, CA: University of California, 1971.

14. Palmer, Bruce, Jr. The 25-Year War: America's Military Role in Vietnam. Lexington, KY: University of Kentucky Press, 1984

15. _____Prisoners of War Achieving Hoi Chanh Status, Circular #1932, Ministry of Defense, Saigon, 1967.

16. Rotter, Andrew. The Path to Vietnam. Ithaca, New York: Cornell University Press, 1987.

17. Salisbury, Harrison E. Vietnam Reconsidered: Lessons from a War. New York: Harper & Row, 1984

With the Dragon's Children

18. Tang, Truong Nhu with David Chanoff and Doan Van Toai. A Viet Cong Memoir. New York: Vintage Books, 1985.

19. _____The Chieu Hoi Program: Questions and Answers, Chieu Hoi Directorate, MACCORDS, Saigon, 1970.

20. Young, Marilyn, The Vietnam Wars: 1945 – 1990, New York: Harper Perennial, 1991.

About The Author:

David J. Garms was born and raised on a farm in southern Minnesota. He received his BA from Gustavus Adolphus College and subsequently joined the Peace Corps, serving two years with an agricultural program in northern India. He received his MPA from the University of the Philippines and PhD from LaSalle University.

After his assignment with AID in Vietnam, he served in Bangladesh, the Philippines, Malawi, Sri Lanka and Italy.

He and his wife, Barbara Carter-Garms, make their permanent residence in Fairfax, Virginia, U.S.A.